JAMIE BUCKINGHAM

PARABLES

Poking Holes In Religious Balloons

Creation House
Lake Mary, Florida

S0-BKK-317

Creation House
Strang Communications Company
600 Rinehart Road
Lake Mary, FL 32746
(407) 333-0600

CONTENTS

FOREWORD

Jamie Buckingham has a gift for painting word pictures that seem so real you could almost live in them. I am very impressed with what he has done with the parables.

Deep in everyone's heart is a desire to know God. From time to time we get a fresh glimpse of Him. But we quickly return to the images we have built from traditions and past experiences. Jamie has removed the veil of those images and helped us see the heart of God.

As I read these parables, I feel as if I know God—how He feels, how much He loves me, how much He wants me to be secure in His love. I especially like the parable of the good Shepherd for this reason.

The apostle Paul said he considered "everything a loss compared to the surpassing greatness of knowing Christ Jesus" (Phil. 3:8). Knowing the Master is certainly your highest goal, as it is mine. And you will meet Him as you read through these parables.

In 2 Corinthians 3:18 we read that "we, who with unveiled faces all reflect the Lord's glory, are being transformed into his likeness."

Thank you, Jamie, for pulling back the veil and letting us see Jesus, for in seeing Him we are transformed into His image.

Marilyn Hickey
Denver, Colorado
February 1991

Not far from where I live in Florida is a mushroom farm. It's really not a farm. It's a big windowless building, the size of a large warehouse. Even though it has a sophisticated environment control system, it is dark and musty-smelling.

Mushrooms, it seems, don't grow well in light. They thrive, however, in a dark, moist, temperature-controlled environment. In fact, the more controlled the environment, the better and more uniform the crop.

Few meals, however, are made totally of mushrooms. This bland, bleached, flavorless, air-filled fungus must be disguised or lumped with something else in order to be enjoyed. This is typical of plants grown in a controlled environment.

Just across the road from the mushroom factory is an orange grove. Oranges, like all citrus, thrive in the open sunshine. Besides that, oranges need a variety of fertilizers, visits by honey bees, water, trimmings and prunings, plus occasional frosts to kill the funguses growing on their branches.

Take it from a native Floridian—there is simply no comparison between a sweet, delicious, juicy navel orange and the bland, gray, musty fungus called a mushroom.

The difference, of course, is sunshine. Oranges grow in the light, mushrooms in the dark.

What does this have to do with the parables of Jesus?

When telling people about God's kingdom, Jesus told stories—stories with meaning. His stories, like oranges, thrived in the light and grew out of real-life situations—many of them tough situations. They were designed not only to be remembered, but to stimulate His listeners to think. Many of His stories closed with a question rather than an answer.

Bottom line: The parables of Jesus were all orange juice—liquid sunshine, we call it in Florida—each glass guaranteed to make you grow. As you read this book, don't gulp. Sip each chapter slowly and learn from the master storyteller.

Jamie Buckingham
Melbourne, Florida

God has many ways of teaching us. Jesus taught by example. Men looked at how He lived and decided to walk that way also.

He also taught by precept. By that I mean He often spoke directly to people. We might even call it preaching.

But His favorite way of teaching was through the use of the parable. He loved to tell stories—stories with spiritual meanings.

In the fall of 1987 I visited Israel with a video camera crew. We had obtained permission from the Israeli government (in fact, had been given press credentials) to set up our video cameras at ten of the sites where Jesus told His best-known parables. There I was to retell, "on location," these marvelous stories. I had long suspected Jesus used visual objects when telling His parables. When He told the story of the good shepherd, He pointed to a shepherd with his flock of sheep in a nearby pasture. When He told the parable of the sower and the seed, He was probably sitting on a rock beside a field where a farmer was sowing his spring seed. Jesus was a man of the earth, and He used earthy things to convey spiritual truth.

For years as a writer, pastor and teacher I wrote, preached and taught about these parables. But on that trip to Israel, visiting the sites where Jesus taught, many things I had never understood began to fall into place.

One evening in Jerusalem I left my American friends who made up the TV production crew and walked through the old city of Jerusalem to the Western Wall, formerly called the Wailing Wall. The Western Wall is the only remaining section of the wall which once encircled the court of the last temple, built by King Herod. It was early October, the closing night of the great Feast of Tabernacles.

All that week, as we had moved through the streets of Jerusalem with our video cameras, we had seen evidence of the ancient Jewish celebration. Every Jewish hotel, business and even many private homes were decorated with a succoth, a palm branch booth symbolizing those forty years in the wilderness with Moses when the Jewish people lived in tents, or "booths" (succoths).

The Feast of Tabernacles, or Booths, is the most sacred and important of the major Hebrew feasts. Solomon was said to have dedicated his temple during Tabernacles. The prophet Zechariah had associated the feast with the coming of the Messiah: "Then the survivors from all the nations that have attacked Jerusalem will go up [to Jerusalem] year after year to worship the King, the Lord Almighty, and to celebrate the Feast of Tabernacles" (Zech. 14:16). It was the only feast that included gentiles—all those who had stood with the Jews across the centuries.

The sun had gone down, and there was just a bit of autumn chill in the air as I made my way through the narrow, winding streets of the old city. My sense of smell was assailed by the ancient odors of spices from the now-closed shops along the way, the smell of donkey dung and an occasional whiff of hashish smoked illegally behind closed doors in old

Turkish water pipes. Virtually nothing seemed to have changed since that day when Jesus walked those same streets, going up to the temple to celebrate the feast with His friends.

Entering the huge enclosure around the Western Wall, I was suddenly jerked back into the twentieth century. Armed Israeli soldiers stopped me at two security points and searched me for weapons or a concealed bomb. But once beyond the gate I was again abruptly thrust back in time. The Jewish rabbis were dancing and celebrating as the Torahs, those ancient scrolls of the first five books of the Bible, were presented to God at the wall.

This was the last day of the feast. Each day of the year the Orthodox Jews had read a prescribed passage of Scripture from the first five books of the Bible—designed so they would read through the Torah and finish on the last day of Tabernacles. In the morning they would start over again, reading through the books of Moses. I stood to one side, watching as a parade of singing, dancing Jews, led by an old, bearded rabbi holding the sacred scroll, came into the area around the Western Wall.

My mind flashed back to a summer afternoon in 1966. I had just walked into the student lounge of the men's dormitory at Southwestern Baptist Theological Seminary in Ft. Worth, Texas. I had re-entered the seminary that summer, eleven years after I had graduated, for an eight-week continuing theological education session. I was going through the darkest period of my own wilderness wandering. Leaving my wife and children in our little rented house in Florida, I had returned as a battered pilgrim to my theological roots, as a lost child yearns to return to his mother's lap, seeking direction for my life.

The television set in the lounge was on, giving the latest news of what was subsequently called the Six-Day War that was being fought in Israel. Several seminary professors were sitting on the edge of their chairs, their eyes glued to the set. "Prophecy is being fulfilled before our eyes," one Old Testament professor whispered in awe. The city of Jerusalem, which had been divided by the Arab occupation, had just been united for the first time since the days of Jesus. Israeli forces had just broken down the barriers which had separated the Jews from the Western Wall for the last two thousand years. Weeping Israelis by the thousands were streaming through the once-barricaded streets, making their way to the former site of the temple. It was a deeply moving experience.

Now, twenty years later, I was there also. Out of my own personal wilderness I had for years been walking in what could only be described as the promised land of God's protection, provision and prosperity. I reached in my pocket and pulled out my little blue and white yarmulka, the Jewish cap which all men are required to wear as head covering when they enter sacred places. Even though I was a gentile Christian, I put it on with honor and made my way toward the wall to pray with my Jewish friends.

Many of the elements of the ancient, beautiful rituals of the Feast of Tabernacles had been lost across the years. In the days of Zechariah, each morning of the seven-day festival a procession of barefoot priests and Levites clad in white linen robes would descend from the temple to the spring of Gihon in the Kidron Valley. (The spring still flows through Hezekiah's tunnel, but the water is no longer accessible until it emerges into the Pool of Siloam.) At the Virgin's Fountain, the officiating priest would fill his golden pitcher with water while a choir of Levites sang the messianic chorus from Isaiah: "Therefore with joy shall you draw water from the wells of salvation, and in that day shall you say 'Praise the Lord!' " (Is. 12:3-4).

All the priests and the worshippers in the procession carried "lulabs," branches of myrtle and willow tied together with palm fronds, in their right hands, and citrons or lemons in their left hands. (The lulabs and lemons were symbolic of the fall harvest.) As they walked, they sang psalms of praise and thanksgiving to the Lord. The procession would ascend to the temple and enter the sacred area through the Water Gate. The priests would march around the huge stone altar once, waving the lulabs and singing, "Save us, we beseech Thee, O Lord, we beseech Thee, give us success." As that was going on, the officiating priest would mount the ramp and pour pitchers of water and wine through silver funnels onto the altar fires.

Each night of the festival the entire temple courtyard would be lit by four huge candelabra called menorahs. For most of the night the celebrants would dance before the menorahs with burning torches, while the Levites chanted psalms accompanied by the haunting music of flutes. At dawn every morning the priests would gather at the Eastern Gate of the temple. As the first rays of the sun peeked over the hills of Moab to the east above the Dead Sea, the priests would turn westward, face the temple sanctuary and chant: "Our fathers when they were in this place turned their faces toward the east, and they worshipped the sun toward the east; but as for us, our eyes are turned [westward] toward the Lord."

Most of that beautiful ritual had been lost during those two thousand years in which the Jews were scattered, barred from their homeland. But some of it had been restored, and I realized I was standing in the middle of one of the most powerful of God's ordained traditions, grafted into my Jewish heritage by my relationship with the Messiah.

The following morning I would take my camera crew to a little balcony overlooking the Western Wall. There, with this same courtyard in the background, I would videotape a short "teaching" from one of Jesus' parables—the parable of the two men who went up to the temple to pray. That night, however, I wanted to forget the project and simply be like the tax collector in that parable who pulled off to one side and knelt before God, crying out, "Be merciful to me, a sinner."

But as I looked around, I realized no one in that huge crowd of thousands of Jews was kneeling. All those praying at the wall were standing, going through various motions and gyrations. I knew that I, as an obvious gentile, was nothing more than a tolerated outsider. I did not want to be conspicuous, nor offensive. Close by I saw a huge fountain where the Orthodox Jews, with their beards and long side curls, dressed in their traditional rabbinical clothing, were washing their hands in ceremonial cleansing before approaching the wall. I was looking for a place where I, too, could pray, apart from the crowd. Turning, I inadvertently bumped into a young Hasidic (ultra-Orthodox) rabbi.

"Gentile dog!" he snarled. Then, without warning, he spit on the front of my shirt. Whirling away, he made his way back to the fountain. Having been touched by a gentile, he felt unclean and was now forced to go through the ritual purification once again.

I had never in my life felt so alone, so rejected. Suddenly I knew how the Jews had felt across the centuries as they had been hunted, persecuted and killed by religious people—both "Christians" and Moslems. Only this time it was I, a follower of Christ, who was the object of contempt— scorned for not being as religious as that young Jewish rabbi. Standing in the midst of that cacophony of religious sound, with spittle running down my shirt, my entire identity changed. I was suddenly at one with the blacks and Indians of America who for generations had been considered less than human—good only as pack animals and objects of social and sexual exploitation. In that moment I was no longer a prominent author, a recognized Christian leader, a person of status. I was

13

instead numbered with the poor, the Hispanics, the mentally ill, the physically handicapped, the prisoners, all minority groups. But most of all I was one with Jesus, who "came unto His own, and His own received Him not" (John 1:11, KJV).

I made my way out of the crowd, never getting to the wall. Back through the security gate I found a dark, quiet corner where a narrow street turned and went up a set of old, worn steps. There, afraid to kneel since I did not know who else might come along and be offended by me, I sat in the darkness and prayed. It was then I began to understand for the first time the meaning of Jesus' parable of the two men who went up to the temple to pray: one proud and haughty, the other despised and hated. How had He done it? How had Jesus been able to rise above personal rejection and tell such a profound story, remarkably combining both satire and pathos? While obviously identifying with the outcast, He humorously used the occasion to poke holes in the balloons of those who were puffed up over their religion. I knew that only as His Spirit filled me would I be able to live free, victorious over the bondage of dead tradition.

As you study these parables of Jesus, may the same Holy Spirit who inspired Jesus in the telling of them work in your own life to give you spiritual understanding. The purpose of this book is not to give serious exposition to the biblical background, nor even to be an expository study of the parables. Others have done—and will do—far better than I in that kind of writing. Rather I've written this little book to stimulate you, excite you, change you by bringing you to the place where you will see that the parables of Jesus were not only for yesterday; they are for today. They were not just for those people who heard Jesus in person—they are for you.

Jesus was a storyteller. He was a master storyteller. Unlike most storytellers, however, He did not tell His stories to entertain. He told His stories to teach. He wanted His listeners to learn about God, about God's kingdom, about God's Son and about themselves. The stories He told were filled with humor, common sense, biting satire and deep spiritual truth. They prodded. They stimulated. They raised questions. They answered questions. But always they pointed the listeners toward God's highest way for their lives.

In this book you'll visit the sites where Jesus actually told these marvelous stories. There I want you to listen with your heart as He still teaches across the centuries.

I want you to stand with me high above the ruins of an ancient inn along the notorious road from Jerusalem to Jericho, where a despised Samaritan stopped to render aid after the religious people had passed by.

I want you to go with me into the bottom of one of those mysterious wadis, or canyons, which crisscross the wilderness regions of southern Israel. It was there Jesus might have stood as He told the story of the two houses—one built on rock and the other on the sand of the canyon bottom.

And I want you to come back with me to the Western Wall and understand, as I am beginning to understand, what Jesus must have had in mind as He told that troublesome story of the two men who went up to the temple to pray—one a Pharisee, another a publican.

Always remember, however, as you read, that the purpose of these parables is to poke holes in our religious balloons—to deflate our own understanding so we can be filled with the spiritual understanding of the Holy Spirit.

You'll meet yourself in every one of these parables. And, it is hoped, the person you see will then call out to God for growth and improvement. For if you are one of those folks like me who are hungry and thirsty for righteousness, these parables will introduce you to the One who will fill you and help you grow.

These ten parables of Jesus—as simple yet profound as they were—are still speaking to the hearts of all those who have "ears to hear," as Jesus was fond of saying. It is my prayer that as you study them you, too, will allow God's Spirit to speak directly to your heart, changing your understanding of God and improving the quality of your life and ministry on earth.

Jamie Buckingham
Melbourne, Florida

ONE

THE PARABLE OF THE TALENTS

Using Our Hidden Gifts
Matthew 25:14-30

For the first time in my life I had invested in mutual funds. A friend, one of the nation's foremost financial advisors, had helped me sort out my priorities. "If you want to play it safe," he said, "put your money in a fund where you can expect steady growth. That way you can leave it alone for a long period of time and not have to worry about it. If that's what you want to do I recommend the Fidelity Freedom Fund.

"On the other hand," he said, "if you are willing to 'work' your fund, follow the stock market every day and perhaps have a spectacular increase in your money, I recommend the Fidelity Overseas Fund—which is the hottest thing going right now."

I thought about what he said. I considered my time, my desires and my rather dismal past record of financial investments. I concluded I should choose the safe (but slow) growth fund.

A year later I was flying back to my home in Florida from the West Coast and picked up a financial magazine on the airplane. Leafing through the pages, I found a full-page ad with a bold-faced headline. "If you had invested $10,000 in the Fidelity Overseas Fund ten months ago, today it would be worth $24,655."

I sat in my seat, staring out the window at passing time and space, and felt the bile of regret welling up inside me. It was the same feeling I had felt the year before when I was in Lebanon and drank something I had been warned could make me horribly nauseated. Only this time I didn't want to vomit; I just wanted to sit and cry.

I recalled John Greenleaf Whittier's lament in "Maud Muller":

> For of all sad words of tongue and pen,
> The saddest are these: "It might have been."

The realization that I could have been wealthy set off a chain reaction of the other mummified regrets I have hugged with me across the years, wrapped corpses of things not done. These are the "Had-I-only-done" things which creep out of the anxiety closet of my mind to haunt me on those rainy, lonely nights when I'm away from home and someone has just told me it's time to face up to my worthlessness.

Had-I-only mortgaged everything I had and invested in the Overseas Fund. At the bottom of the magazine page, in small type, was a disclaimer. "Past performance is no guarantee of future results, and the fund can be volatile." It made no difference. It made no difference that the newspaper that morning showed the Overseas Fund had plunged drastically, and those who didn't have enough financial sense to get out ahead of time had lost millions. All I could think of was that 140 percent increase over ten months.

Had-I-only bought that property next door when my neighbor tried to sell it to me. Today it is worth ten times what it was then.

Had-I-only continued with my piano lessons when I was a boy.

Had-I-only studied Spanish and Russian when I was in college.

Had-I-only not stopped by that woman's house twenty-five years ago.

Had-I-only not put my wife through some of the agony she suffered because of my foolishness.

Had-I-only spent more time with my children when they were small.

I sat for more than an hour feeling sorry for myself, swilling around in the mud and mire of "it might have been." Then a Bible verse flickered through my mind: "...If anyone is in Christ, he is a new creation; the old has gone, the new has come!" (2 Cor. 5:17).

My life was not all minuses. There were some pluses as well.

I remembered my father's balance sheets in his big green ledger books. A true balance sheet includes assets as well as liabilities. Laying down the magazine, I took pad and pen from my briefcase. Pulling down the little tray from the back of the seat in front of me, I made two columns on the yellow paper. One I titled, "Wish I had (or had not)." At the top of the other column I wrote, "Glad I did (or did not)."

I started with the minus column. By the time I finished I had written twelve things. Sure, there were many others I could have dug back and found—things like, "I wish I had not gone fifty-two miles per hour in that forty-miles-per-hour speed zone thirteen years ago." But I had paid the penalty for that (twenty-eight dollars) and learned my lesson. The things I listed were the things I was still paying for. The things that had left scars on me and others.

When I got to the bottom of the list I was feeling considerably better. I leaned back and mused, "That's not so bad for a fifty-five-year-old guy."

Excited, I started on the plus column. The more I wrote, the better I felt. I'm glad I met my wife-to-be when we were in high school. I'm glad I married her and not someone (anyone) else. I'm glad I committed my life to Jesus Christ when I was twenty-one years old. I'm glad I went to a Christian college rather than the state school that offered me a football scholarship. I'm glad I didn't accept the army commission which was offered when I graduated but went on to seminary instead—even though I hated preachers. I'm glad...on and on the list went. Page after page. I was just getting into the list of things I was glad I had given away when the plane landed and I had to stuff my pad back into my briefcase.

I left the magazine on the seat of the plane, still open to the financial ad. With it I left my regrets. I walked down the steps to a loving family and church—a wealthy man. Again I remembered Whittier's comments on poor Maud Muller:

> God pity them both and pity us all,
> Who vainly the dreams of youth recall.

I paraphrased the rest of the poem.

> For of all *glad* words of tongue or pen,
> The gladdest are these: "No regrets."

Surely there can be no more welcome words to fall on the ears of our soul than to reach the end of the line and hear our Master say, "Well done, good and faithful servant...."

Man has been placed on earth as a caretaker of God's business. Each of us has been given a portion of life and charged with the responsibility of taking care of it, increasing it and finally presenting it back to God for His approval.

The final week of His life on earth, Jesus spent a lot of time with His closest friends—trying to teach them about the kingdom of God. He had just finished telling them a parable about some bridesmaids who didn't prepare and missed the wedding. He warned them that tough times were coming and they needed to have spiritual reserves. Then, spotting a caravan leaving the city of Jerusalem, He launched into another story to illustrate the importance of stewardship.

"[The kingdom of God]," He said, "is like a man going on a journey, who called his servants and entrusted his property to them. To one he gave five talents of money, to another two talents, and to another one talent, each according to his ability. Then he went on his journey" (Matt. 25:14-15).

A talent was a measure of weight used by the Greeks, such as an ounce or a pound is a Western weight term. When used to measure silver, it became the term used to describe money. In Jesus' day the term "talent" probably described the amount of silver worth about a thousand dollars in today's market. (A talent of copper would have been worth less, a talent of gold worth more.) The "talent" therefore was the monetary medium, just as today we would say "dollar," "peso," "pound" or "gilder," depending on your national exchange medium.

In the parable Jesus told, the master distributed money to his servants. To one he gave five thousand dollars, to another two thousand dollars, to a final one he entrusted one thousand dollars.

The man who had received the five talents went at once and put his money to work. Perhaps he invested it in Fidelity Overseas, or maybe he bought seed, planted a crop and doubled his resources. When he finished he had doubled his amount and now had ten thousand dollars.

The man with the two talents did the same, doubling his money as well.

But the man who received one thousand dollars was fearful. He dug a hole in the ground and hid his master's money. He wanted to be sure he kept it safe and therefore was afraid to invest in risky ventures.

Sometime later, Jesus continued, the master of those servants returned and settled accounts with them. He commended the two servants who had increased what they had received. In fact, his commendation was the same for the man who had received two talents as for the one who had received five. But he had the harshest condemnation imaginable for the fearful servant who proved to be lacking in innovation, imagination and faith—the one who did nothing more than return to him what he had received, without growth or increase.

The key to this parable is the word "afraid." The two servants who received the master's blessing were daring, adventuresome, willing to risk. But the master severely condemned the final servant for being afraid, telling him the least he could have done was put his talent in an interest-bearing bank account, buy a certificate of deposit or invest it in something safe like the Fidelity Freedom Fund.

But the fellow had done nothing. He just buried his master's legacy in the ground, where it actually lost money on an inflationary market.

"Take the talent from him and give it to the one who has the ten talents. For everyone who has will be given more, and he will have an abundance. Whoever does not have, even what he has will be taken from him. And throw that worthless servant outside, into the darkness, where there will be weeping and gnashing of teeth" (Matt. 25:28-30).

Those words in Jesus' parable used to bother me until I realized the context of the story. Jesus was talking not only to His disciples but to a group of religious people who were standing around listening. These scribes and Pharisees—masters of the Jewish law—were perfectly pictured in Jesus' description of the fearful servant. Fearful of losing the

21

law that God had given them, they had become highly protective. They had taken His wonderful revelation and hidden it away, determined to keep it to the letter. But in the process they had lost all.

God gives everyone the same opportunity. The scribes and Pharisees, however, had made a conscious decision to risk not. Thus, when the master returned and demanded an accounting (and there is always a payday), they had nothing to give God but that which they had received in the first place. In fact, they didn't even have that, for the revelation of God is given for one reason alone—growth and expansion.

God does not want us to keep anything—including the law. Actually, the law keeps us. If all we do is try to keep it, we lose it. We possess only that which we give away.

That which we have is given so that it may be improved upon. Life is not a museum, and we are not charged with being curators of antiquity. God has given us life and His own revelation so we can use our imagination and spirit of adventure (another word for "faith") to expand, improve on, enlarge that which has been entrusted to us.

The whole aim of the scribes and Pharisees was to keep the law exactly as it was. In fact, it was said of the scribes and Pharisees that "they sought to build a fence around the law." The Torah was more important than anything else on earth. They clutched their scrolls, protecting them with their lives. Any change, any alteration, anything new was forbidden.

If the disciples had done with the revelation Jesus gave them what the scribes and Pharisees did with the revelation of Moses, the kingdom of God would have ground to a halt. Jesus gave His revelation and instructed His disciples not to keep it, but to share it. In fact, He literally "commissioned" His followers to "go into all the world and preach the good news to all creation" (Mark 16:15).

The basic purpose of the religionists was to hold on to what God had given them. Their Torah was so precious that no gentile could even look at it, much less touch it. It was kept in a huge silver case, protected from foreign eyes.

Now here comes Jesus, breaking down that concept. He said to His perplexed disciples, "I have other sheep that are not of this sheep pen. I must bring them also. They too will listen to my voice, and there shall be one flock and one shepherd" (John 10:16).

Jesus was saying, "I don't want you to try to protect, preserve or defend the gospel. I want you to risk everything to give it away."

Jesus' purpose on earth was to make all things new, to challenge us to enlarge and expand our concepts, thoughts and minds. But here was a group of people who had paralyzed God's truth by hating anything that was new. "I will not think any new thoughts. I will not take any new action. I will not venture out. I will not explore. I will do only that which I have done, that which is safe."

There can be no spiritual advancement without some kind of risk, some kind of adventure.

I grew up in a denomination that would never allow the people in the churches to hear anyone except a speaker of their own persuasion. No Methodists (they were too liberal), no Episcopalians (they drank wine at communion), no Catholics (they submitted to Rome) and certainly no Pentecostals (they seemed out of control) were allowed behind the pulpit. We were afraid of pollution.

Those ancient scribes and Pharisees were not the only "jot and tittle" people. The legalists, the religionists, the "keepers of the law" remain in our midst. That is the reason this parable is so relevant today. Jesus teaches that we don't have to be afraid of truth, regardless of the clothes it wears, the language it speaks or the culture it comes from. Jesus has sent His Holy Spirit, who enables us to discern that which is truth and that which is falsehood. That is one of the marvelous gifts He gives people: the ability to sort through and spit out the bones and swallow the meat. Even a cow has enough sense to spit out the sticks and swallow the grass.

There are those, for instance, who say: "All psychology is of the devil. All rock music is of the devil. All Catholics are of the devil."

Others say: "All charismatics are of the devil. Stay clear of anyone who speaks in tongues."

There is truth, although not complete truth, in every denomination, in every culture. In every expression of godly worship there are areas of truth. Some worship Him in dance, others in kneeling; some in wild abandonment with clapping and shouting, others in quietness and tears. God merely asks us to open our minds to all things.

When Corrie ten Boom came to our church to speak some years ago, my wife—who had been bombarded from all sides by people who were telling her various ways to cast out demons—went to her.

"Tante Corrie," she asked, "what method do you use to take authority over demons?"

The venerable Dutch saint looked at her with stern face but sparkling eyes and said, "I use whatever method God tells me to use."

The pharisaical approach to ministry is to say, "There is only one way. Close the door on all ways other than my way." Immediately, however, we discover we have shut out every voice except the voice of the past as it is filtered through us. That means we cannot trust anyone except ourselves. Then, when we find we, too, are flawed, we're in big trouble.

There can be no spiritual advance without adventure. God says, "Open your minds." He wants our minds open to truth regardless of the fact that it may cut across our desires, traditions or previous conclusions. Growth comes painfully. Virtue comes only through confrontation—with self, with our adversaries, with God. Beware of people, including yourself, who say, "Don't confront me. Don't ask me questions about what I believe. Don't invade my comfort zone. Leave me alone."

I recently asked our church staff to begin critiquing my sermons. Some were afraid I might react if they disagreed with what I said or how I said it. Others felt it was wrong to criticize their spiritual leader. A few felt uncomfortable critiquing my "words from God" to my face, preferring to do what they had always done—criticize me behind my back. However, when the staff began to realize I not only wanted but needed their input, they slowly began to open up. It was painful to me, but I knew I needed their collective wisdom. I also knew the only way I was going to be able to grow was to be open to confrontation.

Totalitarianism, in government or religion, denies growth and change and destroys individuality. We cannot talk about justice and truth unless we talk about freedom at the same time. Freedom is the cloak that surrounds justice. As an individual I must have the right to think and the freedom to explore. Although I must be open to what others think, I must never let my mind be controlled by anyone else's thinking.

Jesus came to release people to think. The beauty of our walk with Christ is its diversity. If we listen only to those with whom we agree, we will never grow; we will never walk into truth. That is risky, but Jesus teaches in this parable that unless we risk that which He has given us we are in danger of losing all.

Here are eight things this parable teaches:

1. *The giving of spiritual gifts is a sovereign action.*

Remember, Jesus was not talking about money when He used the talent as His medium. He was talking about the things God gives to each one of us. The master in Jesus' parable was not obligated to distribute anything to anyone. He gave freely, but he also gave sovereignly. The servants had no say-so over what they received. That was the master's business. So different people have different gifts. We should never envy another for the gift he has, nor complain about the gift we have (or don't have)—that is God's business.

Several years after Jesus told this parable a man by the name of Paul wrote a letter to the church at Corinth. He went into great detail to explain the gifts of the Holy Spirit—everything from the ability to discern spirits to speaking in tongues. "All these are the work of one and the same Spirit, and he gives them to each one, just as he determines" (1 Cor. 12:11).

God is the One who gives the money, the abilities, the gifts. He does it sovereignly. It is not up to us to question, but to rejoice and put to use that which He gives us, so we may present it back to Him with increase "in the time of accounting."

2. *Everyone receives something. Nobody is excluded.*

Everybody in the kingdom of God has been blessed by God with certain abilities, talents, resources. There is no one who can truthfully say, "I have received nothing from God. I am not worth anything." Each of us has worth, and each of us has ability. "Now to each one the manifestation of the Spirit is given for the common good" (1 Cor. 12:7).

One woman recently spoke to me in my home. Her husband had left her to live with another woman. Since she was in poor health and unable to work, her only source of income was government welfare and an occasional child-support check from him. She was living in a dingy trailer in a drug-infested subdivision. She felt God had passed her by when the gifts were handed out.

"Where is your son?" I asked.

"He's finishing his third year of college," she said.

"How is he paying his tuition?"

"I give him a few dollars each month, and he works late at night in a pizza restaurant to earn the rest."

We sat quietly for a few moments. Then she smiled for the first time. "He is a great gift to me."

"And you are a great gift to him," I reminded her.

The purpose of gifts, great and small, is that they may be used to help someone else.

Our son Tim was born with some kind of mysterious learning disability. He finally made it to junior high school, with seemingly little chance to pass his courses. But God had given a gift to a woman in our church named Edna Hunt. She stepped forward and said, "I am supposed to tutor your son every afternoon after school." She did that for a year, meeting him in one of the back rooms in our church building. She took his assignments from school and with painstaking effort walked him through each one. Under her tutoring we watched Tim gradually improve until he was able to pass all his classes and enter high school.

When Edna's husband, Norv, was transferred out of town, my son was left alone, floundering in a huge high school. The very first week he was there he was attacked by a senior boy. He fought back, defending himself. The principal suspended both boys for two weeks. Tim was devastated. There seemed to be no way he could ever catch up, much less graduate. Then a man named Tom Law, a teacher in the high school, approached us. "I've watched your son," he said. "He has great potential. I want to give him what I have." For almost three years Tom used his gift to tutor Tim after school and on weekends. Tim not only graduated, but went on to complete a two-year college course in agriculture and farm management.

Everyone has received something precious. As we invest what we have—no matter how small—God gives the increase and the blessing: "Well done, good and faithful servant...."

No one can say he is not important. Everyone has worth and importance. The only person who is worthless is the one who refuses to invest his gift in others, keeping it only for himself.

3. *God gives each of us differing gifts.*

It's not the gift that matters, but how we use it. God never demands from us abilities we don't have. He never asks us to do something He has not gifted us to do. If He asks us to do something, He has either given the gift already or is getting ready to give it as we obey. He will never ask us to do something we cannot do.

Our problem arises when we try to equate our gifts with those others have received. If only I could sing as she sings.... If only I could speak as he speaks.... If only I had the administrative skills of that person.... If only I had enough money to....

But it is not what we have that matters; rather it is how we use it. Once we understand that, life becomes peaceful. Once we understand God is in control of our lives, that He wants us to do only that which we can do, then we can be happy in what we are doing. This removes the threat of competition. I don't have to win. All I have to do is obey.

God never demands from us abilities we don't have. We demand that of ourselves. Or we demand it of one another. But God never does. All He wants us to do is to use fully all He has given us.

To be sure, there are things life demands of us which we don't feel called to do—but we can do them. These are the mandatory things in life. Either no one else will do them, or there is no one else to do them but us.

I don't think, for instance, that I am especially gifted to carry out the garbage. But I have to do it, now more than ever. When my children were living at home, I could command them to do it. (They protested loudly that they were not gifted in that area either; I reminded them of the difference between a gift and a call—my call.) Now that they are gone, I do it because I don't want to be inundated with garbage.

On the other hand, I know a man who stops by his invalid neighbor's house three times a week just to empty his garbage. He tells me of the great joy he has in fulfilling his gift in life: taking out his neighbor's garbage.

No one is equal in talents, but all of us can be equal in effort. My oldest son, Bruce, breezed through high school and college, worked in Congress as a legislative assistant for seven years and then took a job with NASA in public relations. He's a "white-collar" man. My younger son, Tim, after struggling through school, secured a "blue-collar" job. He has a strong body, enjoys outside work and is gifted with animals. Both are wise beyond their years and are excellent storytellers. Bruce, however, is a writer. Tim is a talker.

Is one worth more than the other? Absolutely not. It's just that each has different gifts.

All God asks of us is that we do our best with what we have received.

4. *The number of talents distributed to each servant is unequal.*

In this parable Jesus points out that some people are more "talented" than others.

I have taught my children that maturity begins when they realize two things. First: This is an unjust world in which we live. Nobody is going to treat you fairly. This world is going to take advantage of you every chance it gets. Planet Earth is a bad neighborhood. This world is populated with people who will kill you to save their own lives, who will lie about you to get an advancement, who will steal your money and pollute your children with their filth. To say "But it isn't fair" is simply to reveal your immaturity.

The second realization which marks the beginning of maturity is this: Somebody can always do it better than you can. The quicker you realize that, I tell my children, the less frustrated and dissatisfied you will be.

I've always wanted to be the best at something. But every time I think I've arrived, I look up to see there is a long line of people who have gotten there before me. When I reached the conclusion "I'll never catch up with them; there will always be somebody who can do it better than I can," life became fun rather than competitive. I didn't have to win. I just had to volunteer to play. God is not calling me to be the best—He's just calling me to give my best.

Like it or not, some are more talented than others. There is nothing wrong with that. We are not all the same. If we were, we would have no need for anyone else.

On the other hand, no one shows up on earth empty-handed either. Each one's contribution is important to the body of Christ, just as each organ is vital to the human body.

We must not think we can do, or are expected to do, what every other Christian can accomplish. I used to be intimidated by people who were more talented than I am. That was because I felt others would think less of me unless I could excel. I did not know that my worth in life is not judged by God, nor by my true friends, based on what I accomplish. I am judged on who I am.

Nor is my worth judged on how well someone else does something. That is not a true standard of measurement. There will always be someone who can do it better than you. You will never be the best at anything. And even if you become the single master of something, it will only be for a season. Ask golf pro Arnold Palmer, once the finest golfer in the world—but no longer. And the new king will soon be dethroned as well.

This realization is never an excuse for laziness. God equates laziness with wickedness. Each believer is commanded to pursue his or her role in the kingdom of God with great diligence—not to surpass anyone else, but to please God. We are judged not only by the degree to which we use our talents, but by the degree that we make it possible for others to use their talents also. When that is done, the kingdom is satisfied.

28

5. *The distribution of gifts is based upon each person's ability to manage.*

As we prove ourselves to be capable managers, we receive more. The reason we do not have more is often based on our unwillingness to manage what we do have. Thus it is important to note that the gifts were given to the servants "each according to his ability" to manage.

This is at the heart of Jesus' teaching. When we understand that, we can also understand the troublesome statement at the close of the parable: "For everyone who has will be given more, and he will have an abundance. Whoever does not have, even what he has will be taken from him" (Matt. 25:29). In short, the distribution of the talents was based on each person's ability to manage them. As we prove ourselves capable managers, we receive more. If we do not manage what has been given us, we lose it.

Everybody has enough. But you will never receive more until you do what God wants you to do with what you have.

How easy it is to say, "If they would only let me," blaming "they" for our problems. "They" become the culprit. Yet in truth we are responsible for ourselves. If you want to be over a ministry, I tell those frustrated "shepherds" in my congregation, then start with a tiny ministry. If you want to be known as a worldwide evangelist, start with your neighborhood. If you want to be blessed by God as a rich man, then use every penny you have to His glory—for the principle of true stewardship lies in the fact that God wants you to be a pipeline of His riches to others, not a purse for yourself.

For that reason I have become extremely careful of what I do with my money and my time. To blow my money on worthless entertainment, luxurious items with no more practical value than less expensive items, expensive meals which are far less nutritional than plain food, travel junkets and other time-wasters is to put myself in a position to hear God say, "Take the talent from him...."

I have been charged as a manager over my body, my time and my money, just as surely as those servants were charged to invest their talents for the master's glory. I am called to justify every expenditure by God's economy. That is good management.

6. *The reward of work well done is more work to do.*

The two servants who did well were not told, "Now you can lean back, take your ease, eat, drink and be merry." The master did not say, "Well done, good and faithful servant. You have been faithful in a few things, now you can go into retirement." Instead, they were given greater tasks, greater responsibilities. The reward of work well done is not rest—it is more work.

Only the lazy retire. The people I hear saying, "I can hardly wait till retirement," are lazy people. They are lazy now. People do not retire and become lazy. Rather retirement is proof of their basic laziness.

This does not mean you will not grow older and slow down. Of course you will. You may leave a job and go into something else. You may be forced out of your job because of your age or disability. But God's people never retire from kingdom activity. No true minister of the gospel can ever retire from ministry.

How do you lay down a mantle God has laid on you? You can't do it. It does not please God to burn your candle at both ends, but it is less pleasing to blow it out at age sixty-five. As one man said, "I'd rather burn out than rust out."

A friend asked me what was a good time to retire. I told him, "About two weeks. Then go back to work serving God."

The harder you work, the more responsibility you have. That is part of the whole management scheme Jesus is talking about. If you use what you have and use it well, if you get involved in whatever your hand finds to do and do it with all your might, more doors will open. I know many who were retired from their jobs who are busier now, and far more productive now, than they ever were while they were shackled to their eight-hour-a-day task.

Work is not a curse. Work is a blessing. Happy is the person who answers the call to industriousness. Notice how the master in Jesus' parable equates work with God. "Come and share your master's happiness," the storyteller says of God. God is a busy God. Somehow we have gotten a picture of God lolling around heaven in a big hammock, fanned by angels and eating bon-bons. But He is not like that. He is a God of industry, a God of creativity, a God of work. His work did not stop on Friday night after He made the earth. Rather, after a sabbath day of rest, He cranked up again—just as He expects us to do. Laziness is the curse; work is the blessing. Thus, when we do our jobs well we are rewarded with more blessings.

For that reason, even though I am now convinced I should be keeping the sabbath as a day of rest and relaxation and should deliberately plan vacations and rest times for the sake of my mind, body and spirit, I have struck the word "retirement" from my vocabulary. I plan to work right up until the time God calls me home. To do any less would place me out of God's will.

7. *The man who is punished is the man who will not try.*

Although often used by the Old Testament prophets, the word "wicked" was used only five times by Jesus to describe men. (Twice He spoke of a "wicked" generation, and three times He used the word—sometimes translated "evil"—when describing the devil or his demons.) It's a harsh term of indisputable evil. Yet Jesus used it to describe the man who buried his talent in the ground. He equated it with laziness. He called him a "wicked and lazy servant," and said he would lose not only what had been given him, but he would be cast into the darkness, where there would be "weeping and gnashing of teeth."

Why was this man punished so severely? Because he wouldn't try, wouldn't exercise his faith, wouldn't risk. Fear was the damning influence in his life. Even if he had ventured and lost, Jesus said, God would have blessed him. The lazy servant did absolutely nothing and, therefore, received absolute condemnation.

At the close of a Sunday morning service in our church in Florida, I stepped down off the platform to the table where the communion elements were waiting. After saying a few words of explanation, stating that when we receive the bread and wine in communion, we are receiving Jesus, I asked those who were to serve the elements to the congregation to come forward. Their task was to pass the trays containing the bread and the little individual communion cups among the people.

As I handed the trays to the designated servers, I looked up. Standing before me was a tough-looking fellow with numerous tattoos on his arms. I had never seen him before, but he was there in the line of those waiting to pick up trays. Figuring he was someone who had been designated to serve and I just didn't know about it, I handed him two trays—one holding the broken matzo bread and the other the individual cups. He gave me a strange look but took the trays and walked off with the other servers.

In a moment he was back, standing in front of me with the trays. "Which of these do I eat first?" he whispered.

I realized he was totally unfamiliar with our little tradition. I explained that most people ate the bread first, then drank from the cup.

31

"Should I do that now?" he asked, his nervous hands shaking as he held the trays.

"Why not?" I chuckled. I took the trays and offered him the elements. Gingerly, almost cautiously, he took first a piece of bread, then the cup. "You have just taken Jesus into your body," I smiled, trying to encourage him.

His eyes filled with tears. He was embarrassed and quickly returned to his seat.

After the service was over I saw the same fellow coming toward me. Before I could move he threw his arms around my shoulders and began weeping—loudly. I stood there and held him as he cried. In a few minutes I looked up and saw a woman standing with us.

"I'm his wife," she said, her own eyes filled with tears. "He's so embarrassed. He's never been in a church service in his life. He has been on drugs and alcohol for years. This week he accepted Jesus as his Savior and asked to come to the service this morning. I told him there might be a time when he could come forward and say he had accepted Jesus. When you asked the servers to come forward, he thought that was the time. Then you handed him the communion trays, and he was confused and embarrassed. He didn't know what to do with them."

I stepped back and looked the man in the face. His once-hardened features were soft with tears. "God loves you so much," I said, smiling. "He saw you take that tiny step toward Him and was so overjoyed He placed in your hands the most precious thing the church has—the sacrament of the body and blood of His Son. Then He told you to go give Jesus to other people."

"But I didn't know what I was doing," he wept.

"None of us knows what we're doing. We just obey—and God honors our obedience by blessing us with gifts. The only ones who receive nothing are those who do not step out. There is no 'wrong time' to accept Jesus."

The call of God is always a call to risk.

8. *Finally—and this is the universal rule of life—if a man has a gift and exercises it, God expands it so he can do even more. If he has a gift and fails to exercise it, he loses it.*

This is true of tennis, golf, singing, writing stories or thinking. If you stop thinking, you quickly lose the ability to think. If you stop playing golf and go out on the links twenty years later, you may still know the fundamentals. But when you start to play, you'll discover the edge is gone.

That's what happens when you don't use what you have. The only way to keep a gift is to use it in the service of God and in the service of your fellow man.

In the book I wrote with Congressman/astronaut Bill Nelson called *Mission: An American Congressman's Adventure in Space,* I discovered a basic fact about the function of the human body in zero gravity. The human body is designed to function in an upright position in the gravity field of earth's environment. The moment the human body goes into zero gravity—either in earth orbit or on an extended space journey—the cells of that body begin to deteriorate. The reason: Our bodies are constructed in such a way that exercise is mandatory for health and life. Muscles are designed to work against gravity. The cells of the body are designed to tug against the forces of gravity in what is best described as an isometric exercise. In short, exercise—even if it is nothing more than the heart pumping blood uphill—is necessary for health. Without gravity your cells grow listless, apathetic. Bedridden persons experience this to some degree. People living in zero gravity experience it to the ultimate.

Thus, in space the astronauts have discovered that some kind of isometric exercise is necessary to maintain health while there. On the space shuttle the astronauts use a treadmill for this purpose. Health and life come only through pushing and pulling. Muscles and cells which are not challenged wither and die.

In short: Use it or lose it.

For years I owned an Austrian violin, given me by an aunt who had purchased it in Vienna in 1912. No one had ever played it. When my aunt died a number of years ago, it was willed to me. She had thought one of my daughters might take up the violin. I had it cleaned and restrung and bought a new bow for twenty-four dollars. Then I put it back in the closet, where it remained another twenty-five years.

During a house-cleaning expedition I discovered the old violin. But when I opened the case I found it had deteriorated badly. The gut strings were rotted. The bow, with the price tag still on it, was useless. The violin was covered with mold. The once-beautiful finish was chipping.

The man at the music store who agreed to restore it shook his head. "The moment you put a musical instrument on the shelf," he said, "it begins to decay. This violin had but one purpose in life—to be played daily."

Once restored, I gave the violin to our church so it could be played by those who have the ability but no instrument. For their gift, like the violin, will deteriorate unless they use it to God's glory.

When I think about the judgment, I imagine that once it is established that by faith in Christ we have gained entrance into eternal life, there will be one more question we will have to account for: "What," the Master will ask, "did you do with that which I gave you? What did you do with all those marvelous dreams you had? What did you do with all those gifts?"

When our answer is given, blessed is the person who hears in return: "Well done, good and faithful servant! You have been faithful with a few things; I will put you in charge of many things. Come and share your Master's happiness!"

Father, You have told us to "come and share" in Your happiness. I pray You will excite us and stimulate us and challenge us with Your Holy Spirit. Make us dissatisfied with anything less than excellence—not excellence based on some outside standard, but excellence based on Your Word that we might hear at the end of the line, "Well done, good and faithful servant." Amen!

TWO

THE PARABLE OF THE UNMERCIFUL SERVANT

Forgiveness: The Only Way to Live
Matthew 18:23-35

The parables of Jesus are teaching stories based on fact. Jesus was a master storyteller, and His parables could have been fictional stories. As the original Creator of all the earth, Jesus was a master user of fiction. He had an anointed imagination. No one will ever excel Him in creating stories.

Many people find it hard to believe that God uses the medium of "make-believe." They don't think Jesus ever "made up" anything. But, as Creator, Jesus made up a whole lot of things—including these parables. That is not to say the parables could not have been based on fact. Some of them may have been nothing more than repetitions of true stories. But most of the parables were sheer fancy, coming forth from the anointed imagination of the Son of God.

"Through him all things were made; without him nothing was made that has been made" (John 1:3). When you are the Creator, there is no difference between creating a story and creating a planet, or an animal to go on that planet. Surely the God who created a stately giraffe, a playful kitten, a Charles Dickens and a Bob Hope must have an active imagination.

Jesus loved to tell stories. His stories were not designed to give answers, however, as much as to ask questions. Often He would get a group of hostile, angry religionists together, spin a yarn, then sit back and ask, "Now what do you think of that?" His parables forced people to think and act.

One of the marvelous stories Jesus told was in response to a question somebody asked in an attempt to trap Him. "The Bible says, 'You should love your neighbor as yourself,' " Jesus had just stated. The fellow then asked, "Well, who is my neighbor?" Of course, it was a loaded question, asked by a Jewish Pharisee trying to pin Jesus into a corner. The man wanted Him to say that you don't have to be kind to gentiles; you only have to be kind to Jews. Instead of giving the Pharisee a straight answer, however, Jesus told a little story about a man who went on a journey and was beaten, robbed and left for dead beside the road. He talked about the people who refused to help—and the one person who saved the man's life. Then He answered the Pharisee's question with a question of His own: "Which of these three do you think was a neighbor to the man who fell into the hands of robbers?" (Luke 10:36).

It takes a lot of skill and a lot of courage to raise questions—especially the kind that poke holes in religious balloons. To do that you have to know the right questions. In fact, it's easier to give answers than to ask questions. Men have answers for everything. We grow up in a world that has answers. Newscasters and television commentators know the moment they stick a microphone in front of a person he will spout answers. He may even have answers to questions nobody is asking. Give a man a microphone and he'll tell you stuff you don't want to know—and don't need to know. And he may tell you stuff that isn't so.

Fortunately, Jesus wasn't like that. Jesus loved to slip into the background, ask a few questions, then let the folks answer for themselves. That's what happens in this parable called "The Parable of the Unmerciful Servant." Actually, it was told in response to a question asked by one of Jesus' disciples who was having trouble understanding just what forgiveness was all about.

Jesus had just returned from the Mount of Transfiguration. Some of His disciples had been with Him, and Peter in particular had begun to realize Jesus was no mere teacher. He was the Messiah—the Son of God.

"If your brother sins against you," Jesus had said, "go and show him his fault, just between the two of you. If he listens to you, you have won your brother over. But if he will not listen, take one or two others along, so that 'every matter may be established by the testimony of two or three witnesses.' If he refuses to listen to them, tell it to the church; and if he refuses to listen even to the church, treat him as you would a pagan or a tax collector" (Matt. 18:15-16).

As far as we know Jesus used the word "church" only two times in His ministry. The first time He used it was when He said to Simon Peter, "Upon this rock I will build My church." In this passage He uses the word again, saying the final board of arbitration is the "church."

It is important to keep in mind that the word "church" (Greek—*ecclesia*) did not mean church as we know it today. He was not talking about a building or even an organization. In Jesus' day the church was the ruling council, or the elders of the city. The church was the governing body who sat in the "gates of the city." The word literally means "the called out ones," a group of people who have been appointed, elected or recognized as people with authority; the governing body. Thus, when Jesus said the "church" should be the final arbitrator in disputes, He was not talking about the congregation. He was talking about those with authority, those who ruled.

The entire purpose of this three-step procedure was to bring reconciliation between two people who disagreed.

Then, building on that foundation, He continued, "I tell you the truth, whatever you bind on earth will be bound in heaven, and whatever you loose on earth will be loosed in heaven" (Matt. 18:18).

Unforgiveness, Jesus said, has a binding power. Forgiveness sets people free.

"Again, I tell you that if two of you on earth agree about anything you

37

ask for, it will be done for you by my Father in heaven. For where two or three come together in my name, there am I with them" (Matt. 18:19-20).

Jesus was saying that He is always present, rejoicing and answering prayer, when disagreeing brothers come together in reconciliation.

It was at this point, confused over this new teaching on forgiveness, that Peter asked, "Lord, how many times shall I forgive my brother when he sins against me? Up to seven times?" (Matt. 18:21).

We need to understand the background from which the question was asked. The rabbis taught that you forgave only three times. Rabbi Jose ben Hanina wrote: "He who begs forgiveness from his neighbor must not do so more than three times." Another rabbi, Jose ben Jehuda, said, "If a man commits an offense once, they forgive him; if he commits an offense a second time, they forgive him; if he commits an offense a third time, they forgive him; the fourth time they do not forgive."

That's it. The rabbis' teachings were based on the opening passages of the book of Amos where we find a series of condemnations on the various nations "for three transgressions and for four." The rabbis deduced that since God only forgave three transgressions (after which He let the axe fall), and since man cannot go beyond God, then forgiveness was limited to three episodes.

Confused, Peter asked Jesus: Are You saying we should go beyond the rabbis—even forgiving up to the "perfect number" of seven?

Jesus' answer reveals the nature and heart of God—and the purpose of God for mankind. We are not placed on earth to judge or condemn one another. That is God's business. On the basis of the parable Jesus was about to tell, it is obvious that God is a stern God when it comes to unforgiveness. No, our task is to forgive, forgive, forgive—and let God do the judging.

In His answer, "I tell you, not seven times, but seventy times seven" (Matt. 18:22), Jesus makes it clear there is no limit to the number of times we are to forgive.

The religious legalist will take Jesus' numbers, multiply them out and conclude we are required to forgive 490 times, after which we are justified in drawing our sword and cutting off an ear—or a head. Jesus, however, is talking limitless forgiveness.

Forgiveness, for the Christian, should be a way of life. The Christian never keeps a notebook, adding up merits and demerits. He never says,

"That's it. Now you've gone too far."

Love, Paul tells the Corinthian church, "keeps no record of wrongs" (1 Cor. 13:5). What do you do, however, when the debt that is owed is justified?

A few years ago our little town of Palm Bay, Florida, experienced a deep community trauma. A crazed alcoholic filled his pockets with high-powered ammunition. Then, taking a semi-automatic rifle, he walked into a crowded shopping center and started killing people at random. By the time he was finally chased into a grocery store (where he held a young woman hostage for several hours before the police persuaded him to give up), he had killed six people and wounded a dozen more—some seriously.

Emotions ran high. One of the ladies killed was a sixty-eight-year-old saint who worked in our church nursery. People were confused. What role did justice play in this kind of situation? Forgiveness? Each person had to arrive at his own conclusion. I was proud, however, of Sandy Thompson, the daughter of the slain woman, who made a deliberate decision not to hate.

"If I hate him," she told me, "I am also a murderer. Jesus said: 'Do not murder, and anyone who murders will be subject to judgment. But I tell you that anyone who is angry with his brother will be subject to judgment' (Matt. 5:21-22). He also said: 'You have heard that it was said, "Love your neighbor and hate your enemy." But I tell you: Love your enemies and pray for those who persecute you' (Matt. 5:43-44). Therefore, I have no choice but to love and forgive the man who murdered my mother."

That's what Jesus had in mind when He answered Peter's question, "How many times shall I forgive?" Forgiveness is not something you do, He said in essence; it is a way of life. It is something you are. If you live a forgiving life, you never ask about the limits—for it is as limitless as life itself.

On the basis of that principle, He told this parable about the two servants of the king—both of whom owed debts.

"Therefore, the kingdom of heaven is like a king who wanted to settle accounts with his servants. As he began the settlement, a man who owed him ten thousand talents was brought to him" (Matt. 18:23-24).

A talent of silver was worth approximately a thousand dollars. Ten thousand talents would be close to ten million dollars! Some debt!

"Since he was not able to pay, the master ordered that he and his wife and his children and all that he had be sold to repay the debt" (Matt. 18:25).

Bankruptcy in Jesus' day was not an easy way out. In this case it meant the courts seized not just the man's house, chariot and donkey, but they seized him as well—along with his wife and children. He and his family would be sold on the auction block as slaves.

The man fell to his knees, pleading for mercy. He promised that, given time, he would repay everything.

The king knew this was impossible, and in a magnanimous action, canceled the entire debt and let him go—a free man.

One would think that such a huge forgiveness would bring any man to a place of humility and gratefulness. Not so. Many criminals, pardoned of their crimes, forgiven by the state, leave prison and resume their former way of life. Somehow they believe they are above the law, or since the law sinned against them the first time, they have the right to sin back; or they think the world owes it to them.

I remember working for a book publisher once who fell far behind on his royalty payments to authors. When the authors—some of whom were dependent on their twice-a-year royalty checks to keep them alive—began writing, asking for their money, the publisher went into a rage. He felt he had done them a favor by publishing their books, and despite the contract he had signed with them, they had no right to ask for money.

This is the mentality of the Internal Revenue Service, which often expresses to taxpayers during audits that their money actually belongs to the government, not to them, and they should be grateful the government lets them keep some of it after taxes.

Sadly, I have known many people who were forgiven great sins but were never broken in the forgiveness. They remained proud, haughty, self-righteous, arrogant. God continually warns us against such a spirit. When a man is genuinely forgiven and receives that forgiveness, the spirit of self-righteousness always dies. The problem lies in the fact that many are geniunely forgiven but never receive their forgiveness. Such was the case of the man in Jesus' parable.

"But when that servant went out, he found one of his fellow servants who owed him a hundred denarii. He grabbed him and began to choke him. 'Pay back what you owe me!' he demanded" (Matt. 18:28).

A denarii was worth about nine cents in today's money. Thus, the second servant owed the first man—the man who had just been forgiven a ten-million-dollar debt—approximately nine dollars.

"His fellow servant fell to his knees and begged him, 'Be patient with me, and I will pay you back.' " The second man begged the same thing, using almost exactly the same words that the first man had used to the king. "But he refused. Instead, he went off and had the man thrown into prison until he could pay the debt" (Matt. 18:29-30). When that happened, even the first servant's old friends turned against him. Flabbergasted over his callousness and self-righteousness, they reported the matter to the king.

"Then the master called the servant in. 'You wicked servant,' he said, 'I canceled all that debt of yours because you begged me to. Shouldn't you have had mercy on your fellow servant just as I had on you?' In anger his master turned him over to the jailers to be tortured, until he should pay back all he owed" (Matt. 18:32-34).

That's the end of the story. But it's the wrap-up that drives the point home. Turning to His disciples—those who were the very ones chosen and appointed to carry on His work after He departed—Jesus said: "This is how my heavenly Father will treat each of you unless you forgive your brother from your heart" (Matt. 18:35).

Gasp! In other words, forgiveness is such a serious matter that if we don't forgive; if we live lives of arrogance and self-righteousness; if we are not sensitive to what God has done for us and what we are expected to do for anyone who has sinned against us, we cannot be used by God in His kingdom.

Your life-style has to be a life-style of forgiveness. It is not a matter of numbers; it is a matter of who you are. You are required to walk through this world as a forgiving person. You are not allowed the luxury of building up debits against anyone else. Holding grudges is forbidden.

The man of God, the woman of God, is never allowed to keep a little ledger book in his pocket—or in his heart—where he checks off wrongs against his life.

What, then, do we do with people who have wronged us—genuinely wronged us? What do we do with people who have killed our loved ones? What do we do with a father who deserted us as children? With an uncle or a mother who sexually abused us when we were young? What do we do with someone who has stolen our money? Who has taken that which we earned and promised, "If you give me your money, I will take it and do something wonderful for you and for God"? Then one day we discover our "friend" has gotten in his Rolls Royce and disappeared with the cash, and maybe with our wife also. What do we do?

The world's system says, "Choke him until he pays. Go after him. Get your hands around his neck and choke it out of him."

That was the basis of the Jewish law—the law of retaliation. If he does it to you, do it to him. An eye for an eye and a tooth for a tooth. Even in our Christian culture we say, "Enough is enough. Now it's time to strike back."

These are tough questions. Easy, simplistic answers do not suffice. Just how tough the answers are is found in the life of Jesus, who eventually went to the cross, suffering and dying as He lived out this principle. "Lord, forgive them," He agonized from the cross. "Don't rain Your fire on them. Don't justify Me. Forgive them; they don't know what they are doing."

When we understand salvation, we can understand what Jesus is talking about. Only as we understand the debt that has been paid for us can we grasp how we must treat others who owe us far less than we owe God. Most of us have no concept of what Jesus Christ did for us when He gave His life for us. He canceled out our debt to God. That's what He is referring to here. He paid it Himself. The payment of that debt demanded eternal punishment, for "the wages of sin is death" (Rom. 6:23).

We owed a debt we could not pay;
He paid a debt He did not owe.

The kingdom of God is wrapped up in one sentence from Jesus' Sermon on the Mount, where He sums up the law and the prophets: "In everything, do to others what you would have them do to you" (Matt. 7:12).

Some years ago I had some Christian friends who told me that if I would give them my money, they would invest it and return it to me at a big profit. Instead, they lost it. Not only did they lose it, they squandered it on self. One morning I woke up and realized it was all gone—and they were gone too.

At that point I had a choice: What am I going to do with both debt and debtor? There was nothing I could do about the debt. The money was gone. Wasted. But I could do something about the debtor. I could file a lawsuit, which is what some of my friends advised me to do. "He should pay for what he did, not only to you but to a number of others," they said.

I chose not to put my hands around his neck. "Do not take revenge, my friends," Paul wrote to the Romans, "but leave room for God's wrath, for it is written: 'It is mine to avenge; I will repay,' says the Lord....Do not be overcome by evil, but overcome evil with good" (Rom. 12:19,21).

Therefore, I stepped back, forgave and left the results in God's hands. I never got my money back from the ones who stole it from me, but it has been restored to me—from other sources—in great abundance. And God's wrath, as Paul promised, has been poured out on those who took advantage of me and many other innocent investors in ways that make me shudder.

I am convinced that the reason God restored what I lost, even though it came from totally unrelated sources, is because I didn't go after it. I wanted only what God wanted for me—and wanted it only if I could have it God's way. Besides, the relationship with that brother who sinned against me was worth more than all the money in the world, and because I did not choke him, the relationship was never broken. Then, when the wrath of God did almost consume him, I was able to stand with him as a friend, helping him finally repent and find his own forgiveness. Had I been part of those who took vengeance—and there were many—I could have been disqualified to minister to him. But because I had forgiven both debt and debtor, he owed me nothing, and our relationship remained brother-to-brother.

I cannot afford to wander through this world hating anybody, harboring bitterness, resentment or unforgiveness. To do so would be to open myself to disease and death. It's simply not worth it. One of the secrets to health, happiness and a long life is to be able to say with Will Rogers, "I never met a man I didn't like."

If you give forgiveness, you get forgiveness. If you give judgment, you get it back. Before you put your arms around somebody with a smile on your face and a knife in the other hand, remember there is another person somewhere down the line ready to treat you the same way. Whether you are loved or hated, whether you are forgiven or condemned, depends on whether you love or hate, whether you forgive or seek vengeance. "For in the same way you judge others," Jesus said, "you

43

will be judged, and with the measure you use, it will be measured to you" (Matt. 7:2).

On one of my research trips into the Sinai several years ago I had a small group of men with me. We had been following the footsteps of Moses for almost two weeks. I had made this trip several times before and knew the last night in the desert would be the most significant. This time we camped on the shores of the Gulf of Aqaba, south of the tiny desert village of Ofira. Sitting on the beach around a small campfire under the stars, we reminisced about our two weeks together, expressing our camaraderie, experiencing the sadness that always comes when a beautiful event is ending.

This group of twelve men had never met one another prior to our gathering in New York to fly to Israel. On the first night after arriving in the Sinai, we had camped in the sandstone region near the boundary of the Negev desert. There we had prayed, asking God to let us, during the next two weeks, become "the church in the Sinai."

None of us fully understood what that meant, but we all sensed it meant more than climbing mountains and camping out. We sensed it would mean entering into a relationship with each other, a relationship of love and honesty. What we did not anticipate was the pain we would experience as we arrived at that place of transparency.

Our two Israeli guides, both tough young soldiers who loved the Sinai, became part of our experiment. Although they were much younger than the men in the group, they immediately became part of our "church." Interestingly enough, although this group of American business and professional men—doctors, engineers, lawyers and one minister—were all accustomed to giving orders, they all readily submitted to the authority of our Jewish guides.

On our first day in the desert our guides had outlined some basic principles of the Sinai. "We don't take anything into the desert and leave it," they said. That meant all trash, even orange peelings, would be collected and taken back with us in our desert vehicle.

The other mandate: "We don't take anything out of the desert which we find here." That was hard on several of the men who had come with the anticipation of adding to their rock collections.

That last night, camping on the southern seashore, we spent the night on the beach. After supper, as the tide ebbed, several of us walked out on top of the coral reef that was now exposed. We had our flashlights, examining the beautiful shells and creatures left in the little tidal pools.

When we returned to our camp to make ready for bed, the Methodist minister who was in the group pulled me aside. "I feel ill," he said. "Before we go to sleep would you ask the 'church' to pray for me?"

We did just that. I asked the minister to sit on a rock while the other men stood around, gently touching him with their hands. Our two Israeli guides, although they did not participate, watched respectfully from a distance as we prayed.

When we finished, the man pulled me aside. "I'm sick because I've sinned," he whispered.

"God doesn't make you sick just because you sin," I answered. "If that were the case, we'd all be sick all the time."

"You don't understand," he replied. "Amir, our guide, told us not to take anything out of the desert. Tonight I found a beautiful seashell on the beach and tucked it away in my duffle bag. The moment I hid it my chest began to hurt."

"Well, why don't you just throw it back into the sea?"

"It's more than that. I deliberately broke one of the laws. I need to confess to Amir."

I went with the man as he got his seashell. (It was indeed a beautiful pronged shell of many colors.) Handing it to Amir, who was sitting cross-legged in the sand smoking a cigarette, the minister made his confession.

"It seems you need to tell this story to your 'church,' " the young guide said wisely.

I looked at the man. He swallowed hard but nodded in agreement. A few minutes later I had rounded up the men again and we were back at the campfire. I related all that had happened. Then I pointed to the minister, who was sitting, head down, as part of the circle of men around the fire. "What should we do with a man like this? He is a thief who has broken covenant with the church. He has been rebellious against authority. He has lied and tried to get away with his sin. Now, however, he has come and confessed. What should the church do with him?"

No one spoke. As I looked around the ring of men—desert comrades seated on the sand with the reflection of the small campfire flickering on their faces—I saw every head bowed in shame.

"Since no one has an answer, I'll let Amir settle it," I said. Turning to the young guide, who was standing just outside the circle in genuine interest, I asked, "What should the church do with this thief who has stolen this seashell?"

"You have three options," he said in typical Jewish fashion. "For one, you could ask him to do penance."

"That is the Catholic position," I said.

He grinned and continued, "Or you could put him out of the camp."

"That's the position of the evangelicals and Pentecostals."

"But it seems you can't do anything unless you know his heart."

"That, I suspect, is God's position," I said.

I looked around the group. All heads were nodding.

"Do you believe our brother has genuinely repented?" I asked.

All nodded.

"How are your chest pains?" I asked, looking at the minister.

"They're gone," he said seriously. "They disappeared when I gave the shell back to Amir."

"Then that settles the matter. Let's go to bed."

"Not quite." It was the medical doctor in our group who had spoken.

"What do you mean?"

"Well," he said sheepishly, standing to his feet, "I have a seashell in my bag also."

Another man raised his hand. "I don't have any seashells, but I've been collecting rocks from the first day."

We went around the circle of men. Everyone in the group had stolen something from the desert. They had squirreled the rocks and shells away in their bags or stuffed them into their extra shoes with the intent of taking them back home as souvenirs. The entire church was a den of thieves.

The men returned to where they had laid out their gear for the night, got their stolen goods and brought them back to the campfire. The rocks made a rather sizable pile on the sand. On top of them I laid the dried plants I had picked and hidden—intending to smuggle them back home.

As we discussed the situation we found there was some confusion about the law. The junior guide had said, "Take nothing." Amir, our senior guide, had said, "Take nothing unless you check with me." Our "church," like most churches, had received conflicting directions and was confused by the law.

"What is right and what is wrong?" an attorney in the group asked.

"Since the law is unclear, why don't we keep the small stones and return the larger ones to the desert?" one of the men said.

"Are your stones large or small?" I asked.

He grinned. "Fortunately, all of mine are small, so I can keep them."

"Then you are making up laws to suit your own needs," I said.

He nodded sheepishly.

"We can settle the matter easily," an engineer said. "All we have to do is measure the stones. Let's say anything over an inch in diameter is to be left behind."

I looked over at our two Jewish guides. They were grinning. "Now you sound like my ancestors," Amir said. "It's not enough for God to give a law that speaks to the heart. Now you are writing a Talmud to explain the law. Next you will need a Sanhedrin to decide which shells are big and which are little."

What had started as a matter of the heart had quickly become legalistic and mechanical as we looked for ways to do what we wanted, rather than searching to find what God intended. We finally decided the matter was too weighty for us to determine. By common consent we resolved that each man would have to decide for himself and leave the final judgment in the hands of God.

I think this is what Jesus had in mind when He said it is not for man to judge. Man's task is to forgive one another—for all have sinned—and let God do the judging.

I suspect that if mankind is going to survive, it will not be because we have gotten rid of the fellows who have stolen the big shells while keeping the fellows who have stolen only little shells. Nor are we going to survive by expanding on God's law (which is written on the hearts of His children) and setting up even more rules which none of us can really keep.

We will not survive because we believe the same way, nor because we behave the same way. We will survive only as we are filled with God's Spirit, looking upon each other's hearts as God looks—forgiving one another as God, for Christ's sake, has forgiven us.

Much of our ability to forgive depends on our self-worth. Do we know who we really are: men and women who have been forgiven? Paul wrote the Christians in Colosse: "Once you were alienated from God and were enemies in your minds because of your evil behavior. But now he has reconciled you by Christ's physical body through death to present you holy in his sight, without blemish and free from accusation....and you have been given fullness in Christ, who is the head over every power and authority" (Col. 1:21-22; 2:10).

Based on that principle, I suggest you repeat this little affirmation on a daily basis.

I am deeply loved by God.
I am fully accepted by God.
I am made perfect by Christ.

Father, so fill me with Your Spirit that I may forgive as Jesus forgave, love as Jesus loved and live as Jesus lived. Amen.

THREE

THE PARABLE OF THE TWO HOUSES

High Living in Tough Places
Matthew 7:24-27

The most famous sermon ever preached is called the Sermon on the Mount. It is found in Matthew 5-7. Portions are repeated in Luke 6, 11 and 12. Most Bible scholars agree, however, that the content of the sermon is a compilation of a number of Jesus' teachings, gathered together by Matthew into one discourse.

The "sermon" in Matthew begins with groups of proverbs, called beatitudes. This is followed by several small parables about salt and lamps. Then Jesus takes a number of Old Testament teachings and elaborates on them—giving the words new intent and meaning.

He says, for instance, that while the law states you should not murder, the intent of God is that you should not hate. In fact, you ought to love each other as you love yourself—doing unto others as you would have them do unto you. That "golden rule" sums up all the teachings of Moses and the prophets, Jesus said.

The scribes and Pharisees were offended over the meaning Jesus gave to the ancient laws. When Jesus talked about adultery, He said the real question was not what you do with your body, but what was the condition of your heart. While the scribes and Pharisees judged only on whether sexual intercourse had taken place, Jesus said God made His judgment based on whether we lusted or not. Jesus did not condone sexual looseness; instead, He asked His followers to understand why the law forbidding it had been written in the first place. God wanted men and women to live together in faithfulness in marriage, with hearts so pure toward God that they would desire only their marriage partner.

The central message of the Sermon on the Mount—indeed, the central message of the Bible—can be stated in four words: "the kingdom of God." This term refers to the sphere of God's rule, which embraces all of creation. However, in the Sermon on the Mount Jesus limited His teachings to the kingdom as it relates specifically to God's loyal subjects. Thus, it is necessary to remember that this "sermon" was not preached to the general populace but to Jesus' disciples. Note the opening verses: "Now when he saw the crowds, he went up on a mountainside and sat down. His disciples came to him, and he began to teach them, saying..." (Matt. 5:1-2). The antecedent of "them" is the disciples, not the crowds.

Jesus begins the final portion of this lesson to His disciples by reminding them the human race is divided into two groups—a large group which goes the way of the world, and a much smaller group whose members are subjects of God's kingdom and choose to do God's will. Then He analyzes some of those who presumably have taken the narrow route and finds in the ranks certain "false prophets," leaders who say one thing but do another. Then, in a deeper examination of the small group, He points out "foolish" persons—those who know what to do but choose otherwise. To them He addresses the final parable of the Sermon on the Mount.

Crisis reveals character.

One night I was sleeping soundly in my upstairs bedroom when I heard someone outside in our front yard calling my name. I glanced at my clock. It was 2:00 A.M. I went down and opened the door. A young couple, Debbi and Paul, friends of ours for many years who live across the street, were standing there, grief stricken. They had just returned from the hospital. Both of Debbi's parents had just been killed in an automobile accident.

Debbi poured out the details. Her mom and dad had been driving down a city street when they were hit by a drunken driver going more than one hundred miles per hour. They had been killed instantly.

"As I stood there looking at their bodies," Debbi wept, "I knew God had power and authority over all things—even the power to raise the dead. I begged Him to raise them up, but nothing happened. They're gone."

She wept for a while, then finally looked up. "Was I wrong to pray that way?"

"Absolutely not!" I replied. "There are some things we do not know. We don't know why God allowed this to happen. Nor do we know why God didn't raise them from the dead when you asked Him to. But I do know, beyond doubt, that it was right to ask Him. Instead of cursing God, as some would do, or instead of growing depressed, you exhibited great faith. That pleases God, for it revealed your true nature."

Life is full of crises. Loved ones die or are murdered. Sickness comes. Accidents. Disappointments. Financial ruin. Court decisions. Incarceration. Beatings. Threats. Lost opportunities. Jesus told this parable of the two houses in Matthew 7 to let us know that storms and high water come into every life. When the water rises, you discover whether your house is built on sand or rock. In Debbi's case, her heart was firmly planted on the rock of Jesus Christ.

"I thank God that your first thought was a thought for a miracle," I told her.

The nation of Israel, as with most Middle East nations, is arid. In fact, a great part of the nation is desert—including nearly all the mountainous region in the south.

Jesus spent a great deal of time in what is known as the Judean wilderness, a wild, forboding desert that stretches from Jerusalem to Jericho and on down to the Dead Sea, the lowest point on earth. It is a barren area of mountains and deep canyons. Nothing grows there but a few desert shrubs. It was in this wilderness that Jesus was tempted by Satan, following His baptism in the Jordan River. Several years ago Episcopal Bishop James Pike, his mind strangely twisted from numerous seances and experiences with the occult, wandered through the Judean wilderness with his wife. Lost and disoriented, he fell into a deep canyon. His body was not found for more than two weeks. Such is the nature of this desolate place.

Few countries can compete with Israel for its amount of sunshine— and its lack of rain. The "rainy season" is November through April. May through October may be completely dry. For a number of years the Jews have placed a great emphasis on planting trees, for trees not only hold (and produce) vital topsoil for agriculture but actually bring on the rain. The leaves of trees put oxygen into the air. Oxygen mixes with the natural hydrogen in the atmosphere and forms clouds, which bring rain.

However, in the desert regions of the Judean wilderness, trees won't grow. Rainfall is less than three inches a year. The problem is that it may not rain for three years—then it rains nine inches all at once. When that happens, disaster takes place. The wilderness, where the mountains jut upward from the desert floor, is divided only by mysterious dried riverbeds called wadis. The wadis, or "washes," as they are known as in the American Southwest, are deep canyons with sandy bottoms. They stay dry most of the year, but when it rains in the highlands, the water cascades down the desert mountains, running in torrents over the hard, alkaline soil which absorbs virtually nothing, and eventually spills into the wadis. Almost instantly what was a dry, sandy canyon becomes a raging river. Everything in front of it is swept away. Destroyed. Racing wildly downhill, this wall of water is finally dumped into the Dead Sea—thirteen hundred feet below sea level.

Travelers in Israel are familiar with certain road signs warning of the danger of flash floods in the low areas. Last year three young people ignored one of these signs at a depression in a shallow wadi near the Dead Sea. There were only a few inches of water across the road when they drove their car into the depression. But in seconds it had become a raging torrent, and their car was swept away into the Dead Sea. All three drowned.

I was in the Sinai Peninsula the day after such a wild rainstorm. An entire Bedouin village of tents, camels and even two pick-up trucks had been washed into the Gulf of Aqaba. The Bedouins knew better than to pitch a permanent tent in a wadi, but thought it was safe to pitch them on the alluvial plain, or delta, at the mouth of the wadi where it emptied into the gulf. That was a mistake. A wall of water six feet high came roaring out of the wadi, sweeping away everything in its path. Several people died.

Jesus had all this in mind when He told His disciples this parable about the two builders—one wise, the other foolish.

I like to picture Jesus walking through one of those Israeli wadis, talking with His disciples. "You have a choice where you will build your life," He says. "The lazy man would find it easy to pitch his tent on this soft, inviting sand. It's easy to build here. These wadis stay dry nearly all year long. They have beautiful, flat, sandy bottoms. No land to clear. No foundations to dig. Just pitch your tent, drive in your tent pegs and you have instant shelter. Then pray it doesn't rain.

"But the wise man knows it will rain. Maybe not tonight. Or tomorrow. Or for the next year. But one day it will rain. One day God will demand an accounting."

As the old preacher used to say, payday someday.

The wise man knows the rains will come, so he builds on the mountainside. He finds a rocky ledge, high above the bottom of the wadi, and builds for the future. If you were to follow Wadi Kelt down from Jerusalem toward Jericho, you would come to St. George's Monastery, built by Greek monks hundreds of years ago. It is accessible only from the north side of the deep canyon. It took many years to fasten the foundation firmly on the solid granite of the sheer precipice, but the monks knew the value of building on the rock—high above the easy sands of the wadi floor.

It's tough to build up there on the rocky ledges. You have to drill into the rock in order to put down your foundations. One hermit had to carry building materials on his back, or let them down by rope from the high cliffs above, to build his house. But come November and the winter rains, he was glad he did, for everything in the valley below was washed away.

In the Bible rain is usually seen as a sign of blessing. However, in Jesus' parable the rain created a disaster because the contractor did not build correctly. What was a blessing to one man turned out to be a curse to another because he built his house—his life—on the wrong spot.

According to Jesus' parable, everyone builds some kind of house. In the kingdom of God there are no renters, no sidewalk people. Everyone puts down some sort of foundation. The house represents our character, our life-style, our goals, our dreams, our behavior. There is no way to be non-decisive about our life's house.

So many people live just for today. They never pause to think of the results of their actions, of what might happen tomorrow. Jesus wants us to build our lives for the long haul rather than sacrifice ourselves for the pleasures of today.

Recently I read a remarkable article by George Leonard, one of America's top akkido masters—a sixty-eight-year-old instructor in the martial arts. He was commenting on this principle of people who are afraid to plan for the future, who want everything today.

He said, "We are an impatient society, dedicated to the quick fix. There are signs of it everywhere. Look at the television commercials, and you see they are mostly little moments of ecstasy. You see people getting the reward without doing the work. The rise in the use of drugs can be attributed to this also. For ten years I have run an akkido school near San Francisco. I've had the striking experience of watching students show up the first day with excited eyes, only to drop out quickly at an alarming rate. Only 1 or 2 percent make it to the black belt. Most of the casualties are young men who are mainly concerned with looking good. They are usually preoccupied with overnight progress, with getting ahead without the necessary long-term practice. Watching them fizzle, I keep visualizing the classic learning curve from psychology, and I realize how lost the concept is on most of us. What the average person doesn't understand is that we are learning all the time. Even if it doesn't feel like it, even if it doesn't feel like we are getting anywhere, we are learning."

That's what Jesus was talking about when He said: "Everyone who hears these words of mine and puts them into practice is like a wise man who built his house on the rock" (Matt. 7:24).

Solid-rock living is hearing God and doing what He says. Solid-rock living is building for the future, with eternity's values in view.

One Saturday afternoon I was sitting in my house talking with Major General Jerry Curry, then on active duty with the United States Army. General Curry, a longtime friend, had spent the weekend with us and was to speak in our church the next day. As we chatted, the phone rang. It was a young divorcee I had known for several years. Her eleven-year-old son, a victim of leukemia, was being rushed to the hospital. She was afraid he was not going to live and wanted me to meet her in the emergency room.

General Curry wanted to accompany me. We rushed into the emergency room of the hospital, but it was too late. The little boy's body, mottled from the horrible disease, was lying on a stretcher in a tiny, curtained cubicle. His beautiful mother, a model by trade, was standing at the end of the table, weeping.

Like Debbi, she was exhibiting her faith. "I know God can raise him from the dead," she cried.

Then, looking at me, she said, "God has given you the authority to speak life back into his body!"

"You are right," I answered. "I do have that authority. God has given it to me. But I can only speak what God wants me to speak."

"Will you take authority over death and command life to come back into his body?" she asked defiantly.

"I will if God tells me to do so," I said.

"Will you ask Him? Now?"

"I will," I answered.

I stood there on one side of the little boy's body, still warm from life. General Curry stood on the other side. We stood for a half-hour, waiting for God to speak.

"If God gives you a word," I told General Curry, "speak it. If He gives me permission, I am ready to rebuke death and command him to rise up."

I have never been as ready to shout at death, to do whatever was necessary to see life restored. I could hear the nurses behind the curtain whispering, "There are a couple of crazy men in there, believing they can raise that boy from the dead." It made no difference. I forgot about my image, about public opinion. If God spoke, I was going to speak.

But for reasons beyond human comprehension, God remained silent. We waited, then prayed with the mother and left her in the arms of friends and relatives.

On the way home General Curry and I were silent, each occupied with our own thoughts. I kept asking God why. Why not?

While He had not spoken in the hospital, I now felt I heard His silent voice deep in my heart: "You are in this for the long haul. It's not just for the glory of the moment that you are in this walk, but for the entire march. You need to understand that I am the God of eternity. You can't always have your way, for My ways are higher than your ways. Only one

55

thing is sure—I will always have My way."

The wise person is willing to wait on God. He knows there will be a tomorrow, and a tomorrow, and a tomorrow. He also knows he needs to hear God today in order to be ready for tomorrow.

I recalled the "miracle" that happened one summer near our pasture fence. A huge plant grew up almost overnight. I first noticed it in June as its broad green leaves towered above the pasture grass. By the end of July it was more than six feet tall with a trunk as big around as my wrist. If ever a plant had an "anointing," this one did.

One September afternoon I was helping my son string barbed wire, and we came to the miracle plant. But when I brushed against it, it fell over. I checked it out and discovered it had no substance. It looked big and strong, but it was made of some kind of fluffy fiber. It had a crusty bark, but the interior was mostly air.

No anointing. All puff.

The problem, I discovered, was it had no root system. It just went down into the ground about two inches, where there was a wad of fibers about the size of my fist. When the summer rains had ceased and the water level in the ground had dropped, the plant had died. It still gave the impression of life, but since there was no surface nourishment, it perished. When I came along and exerted just the smallest stress, it fell over.

The next day my son came along on the tractor mower and ran over it. It disintegrated into nothing. Now it is as though it never was—existing only as a sad memory of the tragedy of fast growth and no foundation.

On the other side of my yard is a row of ornamental palm trees which were planted along the driveway a few years ago. They are still the same height as when they were planted. I mentioned this to the nursery man, and he just grinned.

"You're too impatient," he said. "They know better than to go up until their roots have gone down."

Trees that last, I understand, have as many roots underground as they have branches above ground.

The branches on orange trees, for instance, grow outward only to the extent of the outer limits of their root line—which is one of the reasons they cannot be planted too close together.

Sidney Lanier wrote of this one hundred years ago when he commented on the saltwater marshes near Brunswick, Georgia:

By so many roots as the marshgrass sends in the sod
I will heartily lay me ahold on the greatness of God.

I remember a call from a pastor I've known for a number of years. He advertised that his church was the "fastest-growing church in America." He wanted me to come speak at a giant citywide rally. "We need to draw even more people to our church," he said.

I agreed that God wanted the church to grow. But instead of coming to speak at the big rally, I offered to spend several evenings meeting with his elders and church leaders.

"You need to build relationships. Then, as your church grows, your structure won't topple over on you, as has happened to a number of others," I warned.

He thought that was a waste of time, so I declined his invitation. We talked on, but all he wanted to tell me about was the money flowing in, the packed auditorium, the traveling music groups. My concern was different. Do the people love one another with a covenant love? I asked. Do they trust their leaders? Are they a forgiving people? Do they accept those who are different? Do they welcome sinners into their midst?

What would you do, I asked another pastor, if you discovered that within fifty days from the birth of your church it would grow from 120 timid souls to more than 3,000 Spirit-baptized zealots? I then told him I knew of a church where that happened. It's described in Acts 2. But God had more sense than to forewarn the leaders. So, instead of building a building, they built a church.

I've watched too many lives—too many ministries—sprout rather than grow. I guess it all depends on what you want to produce. It takes forty years to grow an oak tree. But you can have a pumpkin—a big one at that—in three months. The difference: one has substance, and the fiber is tough. The other is big and full of nothing.

It's a matter of roots.

That's what Jesus was talking about when He told this parable. He was warning His disciples, saying, "Don't sacrifice yourself for the pleasures of today; rather make your plans for the long haul."

My wife and I had a strange experience in the Miami airport one afternoon. We were on our way to London for a book dedication. Our way had been paid for the three-day trip. We had flown from our home in Melbourne, Florida, down the coast to Miami. There we were to catch a nonstop flight to Newark, where we would transfer to the international flight. However, our plane was delayed by two hours in Miami. That meant we were going to miss our Newark connection to London. There were no other flights. The best the airline could do was tell us to overnight in Miami and catch the same flight the next day.

Rushing through the Miami airport, going from one ticket counter to the other, I felt my chest tighten up as panic set in. Time was running out. We weren't going to make it.

I finally sat down in a little coffee shop with my wife and said, "What are we so anxious about? We can always go home. We don't have to do this. This is stupid."

She began to laugh. So did I. The whole thing was ridiculous. Besides, 98 percent of the people in London would much rather be in Florida. I went back to the ticket counter and said, "Fly us back to Melbourne. We don't want to go to London after all."

As a result, we had three days at home doing absolutely nothing except the things we wanted to do.

I had learned some things about life. I don't have to do everything I want to do, nor do I have to do everything others want me to do.

That's what this parable is all about, for sooner or later everyone is going to get behind the power curve. Time is going to run out. You're going to get trapped in some Miami airport. You're going to wind up in the emergency room of some hospital looking at the body of a little boy, or the bodies of your parents. When that happens, you are going to have to hear God. If you don't, your house will be washed out to sea with you in it.

George Leonard is right. The plateaus are not ends, they are learning experiences to a greater end—and the journey itself is a learning experience.

In short, the means are always more important than the ends. God is not nearly as interested in whether you accomplish your goals as He is in what you become in the process.

Years ago God spoke to the leaders of our church and said, "Don't go into debt." Hearing that word and obeying it—as Jesus instructed His disciples in this parable—slowed us down. Some people left the church because they did not believe we were growing fast enough. Others were confused. They watched the television ministers, many of whom were millions of dollars in debt, and said, "What's wrong with debt? They do it, and look how successful they are."

Then came the day when the rains fell, the waters rose and the winds began beating against the houses of God. There was a huge scandal in the television ministry in Charlotte, North Carolina. Then another broke out in the television ministry in Baton Rouge, Louisiana. Both these ministries were like that giant weed in my pasture. They had grown up almost overnight, were tens of millions of dollars in debt and had no root system. When the tough times came, they fell.

The income of our church suffered too, as did the income of many other churches around the nation. But since we "owed no man," all we had to do was tighten our belt a few notches and go on.

The rain fell on the just and the unjust. The winds beat on all the houses. But those who had heard Jesus' words and done them weathered the storm. The others "fell with a great crash."

God wants His people to build for the long haul, to build for eternity. He's not talking about buildings; He's talking about relationships—with Him and with His people.

I remember the story of a man and his wife who had walked out on a long dock extending into the Mississippi River at Vicksburg. As they stood there, looking at the vastness of that great river, they heard running footsteps behind them. Here came a man dressed in a coat and tie, running as fast as he could toward the end of the dock. They stepped back as he passed them going full speed. At the end of the dock he increased his speed, gave a mighty yell and took a flying leap toward the opposite bank. He went about fifteen feet and splashed into the water.

Alarmed, the couple raced out to the end and fished the man out of the water.

"What in the world are you doing?" the woman asked the man when he was safely on the dock.

Panting and spitting water, he said, "A man up there on the hill just bet me a million to one I couldn't jump across the Mississippi River. I couldn't stand there and think about those odds without at least trying it."

A lot of the things God has asked us to do seem impossible. Totally impossible. But I praise God for people who are willing to try, willing to jump off the end of the dock. Who knows? You'll never get it done if you don't try. You'll never accomplish anything if you are not willing to run the risk.

"Everyone who hears these words of mine and puts them into practice...." That's solid-rock stuff. That's not fanaticism. That's not weirdoism. That's the solid rock of believing what Jesus said is true. When we hear Him and do what He says, our house will be built on solid rock.

That's the reason little kids have to lead the way into the kingdom of God. We adults have too many reasons why it won't work. So God puts little children around us. They don't know it won't work. They do it because Jesus said to do it—and are blessed.

When I get sick, I call my grandchildren to pray for me. They don't know that God doesn't heal people. They believe He does. So they pray for me, and I get healed.

The teachings of Jesus are the foundation of the world. Any life, any institution, any dream, any nation built on any other foundation except the teachings of Jesus Christ will fail. We have a choice of building on the high, difficult solid rock of the teachings of Jesus, or in the low, easy places in the sand of our own desires, intellect and worldly ways. However, when the storms come—and they will come—only the house on the solid foundation will stand. All the rest will fall, and great disaster will follow.

Let us all be as little children who, without question, hear Your words and do them, Lord.

FOUR

THE PARABLE OF THE FIVE FOOLISH MAIDENS

Reserve Strength for Tough Times
Matthew 25:1-13

This parable and all the other parables in Matthew 25 were taught during the last week of Jesus' life, following His triumphal entry into Jerusalem on what we traditionally call Palm Sunday. During that five-day period Jesus had some significant things to say to His followers—things Jesus had known all along, of course, but waited until just before the end of His earthly life to tell them.

There must have been a great sadness in Jesus' heart when He entered

Jerusalem that last time. Despite all the accolades, the waving palm branches and shouts of "Hosanna! Blessed is He who comes in the name of the Lord!," Jesus knew His earthly life was coming to an end. He knew that by the end of the week His enemies would kill Him.

He knew, but His disciples and friends did not know. During the week, however, things became more and more evident. Jesus seemed to be doing strange things. His disciples were disturbed, trying to interpret His parables, but mystified by most of them. Yet Jesus knew He had only until Thursday night to finish teaching His chosen ones. By Friday morning He would be dying on a cross outside the city. He had some significant things He wanted His disciples to remember, so He told them stories. Even if they did not understand the meaning, they would remember the stories. And one day the Holy Spirit would come in power. When that happened, everything would make sense, for the Spirit would interpret all things to His followers—even as He is doing today.

Most often, during this time, Jesus taught about two things: end times and the kingdom of God. The teachings of Matthew 24 concern the "end of the age." He was preparing His disciples for what was about to happen—as well as giving prophetic insight into what would happen many years later when He would return to earth. While Jesus may have been talking about the events which would precede the end of the world just prior to His second coming, it is also obvious He was talking about the fall of Jerusalem, which took place in 70 A.D. At that time the end of the world as the Jews knew it would come to pass; the nation of Israel would be utterly destroyed, and the Jews, especially the followers of Jesus, would be scattered to the far corners of the earth. Similar things would take place in the time preceding the end of the world.

He began by warning the disciples to watch out for certain things which could deceive them. He told them of certain "signs" which would appear prior to His return: wars and rumors of wars, nation rising against nation—that is, nations once friendly with each other turning on one another in bitter war. Yet in the middle of all this confusion and conflict, Jesus said, the gospel would be preached in the whole world.

This didn't make sense to His disciples. One moment Jesus was telling them His life was almost ended, then He was telling them the gospel would be preached to the whole world. The disciples, who by now believed Jesus really was the Messiah, were also locked into a mentality that the purpose of the Messiah was to set them free from the political and military bondage of the Romans. Even after His crucifixion and resurrection, they asked timidly, "Lord, are you at this time going to restore the kingdom to Israel?" (Acts 1:6). They could not think of the kingdom of God except in terms of a political, earthly kingdom. The concept of a kingdom of the heart was foreign to them.

They began to think, How can the kingdom come on earth if they're going to kill Him? They knew the rumblings. The disciples were not fools. They knew there were all kinds of forces out there trying to get to Jesus. How was all this going to happen? In the natural it seemed there was no way the gospel was going to be preached to the ends of the world unless Jesus was there to preach it. And how were all these other things going to happen unless He was there to make them happen?

In response to these and other questions, Jesus just smiled and told His followers to get ready—that when "the time" was ripe, they would understand. Then He told them this wonderful little story about a Jewish wedding to remind them how important it was to be prepared for what was about to happen.

Jesus was probably standing in the courtyard of a friend's home outside Jerusalem when He spoke. He loved using familiar places and events as situations for teaching. A wedding had taken place in the home the night before.

Jewish law called for weddings to begin on Wednesday—usually in the home of the bride's father, or perhaps his brother. They always lasted more than one day. That evening, after a day of festivities, the bride and her bridesmaids would prepare for the groom's arrival. No one knew exactly when he would come. In fact, it was something of a game to try to guess exactly when the groom would show up to claim his bride. The house was made ready, however, and the bridesmaids would then go out into the courtyard to wait for and greet the groom when he arrived. If the bride was a young woman—a virgin—her bridesmaids were also young virgins who would share the excitement of the bride when her groom finally appeared.

The wedding ceremony would not take place until the groom arrived. It would be preceded by a great feast called the "wedding supper." After dinner and the exchange of vows, the young couple would be escorted through the streets of the city to their new home by the light of flaming torches and with a canopy over their heads. For a week they would maintain an open house and be treated like a king and queen. In a land where there was much poverty, where men had to toil in the earth, pull fishing nets or herd animals for a living; where women did hard physical labor and were looked upon as chattels by the oppressive Roman government, the wedding festivities were a supreme occasion in life.

In Jesus' story it was after dark when word came that the bridegroom was on his way. Ten of the bridesmaids went out to greet him, carrying their little lamps with them to light his way down the road and into the courtyard. Remember, there were no street lights in Jesus' day, so the night would have been pitch black. But the groom was delayed for some reason. The young women sat in the darkness on the side of the path, waiting. They finally fell asleep.

At midnight they heard him coming. Each picked up her lamp, a small pottery bowl with a wick hanging over the edge. Some of the bigger lamps in the houses had several spouts for wicks. All burned olive oil.

Five of the bridesmaids had brought extra oil for their lamps. They took their little scissors and trimmed their wicks—little strings of flax that absorbed the oil. Cutting the carbon from the end of the wicks, they then refilled their lamps from the reserve oil they had brought with them.

The other five had no reserve oil. It is important to note that Jesus did not say they had no oil at all. All had oil in their lamps when they went out to meet the bridegroom. But the wise ones had reserve oil. The foolish ones had only the oil originally in their lamps. They had not brought any jars of additional oil with which to refuel them.

No reserves.

"Give us some oil!" they cried. "The bridegroom is coming, and our lamps are going out."

"No," the others replied, "there may not be enough for both us and you. You'll have to go to those who sell oil and buy some for yourselves."

Now that presented a problem. They had expected the groom at dusk. Now it was midnight. Where do you buy oil in the middle of the night? They rushed off in a panic, hoping to find a merchant still open. Chances are they would have had to run all the way back to their own homes to get extra oil, for to have returned to the bride's house without the groom would have been unthinkable.

But while they were gone, looking for oil, the groom arrived. The five wise maidens escorted him joyfully into the house. The bride's father welcomed them. Then, since it was midnight and the other girls had disappeared—presumably gone back to their homes—he shut and locked the outer gate. It was time for the banquet to begin.

Much later the foolish girls came straggling back, begging the gateman to let them in. He refused and sent them away. They missed out on the festivities because they did not have reserves—did not have the strength and stamina to wait things out.

"Therefore," Jesus said, "keep watch, because you do not know the day or the hour" (Matt. 25:13).

I read this story for years believing Jesus was talking about Christians and non-Christians—that the five wise maidens represented those in the kingdom of God and the five foolish ones outside the kingdom. But that is not the case. Jesus was not talking about five virgins and five prostitutes. All ten of these young women were part of the wedding party. All had oil in their lamps. But some were wise and some were foolish. This is a message to the church—to believers.

Everybody had oil to start with. The lamps were all lighted in the early part of the evening. But Jesus was saying, "It's not enough to be a Christian. You need the reserve of the Holy Spirit as well."

The question this particular parable presents is this: Do I have spiritual reserves? What will happen to me when the crisis comes? Will I stand or will I fall?

The one thing everyone should know about crisis is this: It is always unplanned, unpredictable and mostly beyond our control. We would all like the bridegroom to show up when we announced he would appear. The party is going to start at seven, we announce. But how do you handle things when the bridegroom is five hours—or five millennia—late (according to our time schedule, that is)?

Most people don't like crisis and change. We get nervous when things around us are shaken, when those things we've depended on are taken away. We like things nice and easy. We really would like for the bridegroom to show up when we announced he would.

We are masters at trying to second-guess God. Many times I have sat in committee meetings or with other dreamers like myself and made plans. Then, after the plans were made, we (almost as an afterthought) asked God to bless them. We figured everything out using our intellects, then passed it over to God and asked Him to put the corporate seal of the kingdom of heaven on our effort—like the Good Housekeeping seal of approval.

Yet, as I think back across the years, I can't remember a single time in my life when God has honored that procedure. God's way is not for us to reveal our plan to Him and ask Him to bless it; it is for us to present ourselves to Him so He can reveal His plan to us. Our task is merely to obey.

This was the picture Jesus was painting for His disciples when He told the story of the foolish maidens. They were disturbed when the bridegroom didn't arrive on their time schedule—and angry when they were not admitted to the feast. But Jesus was pointing out that God is God. Things not done God's way are never blessed.

God has a way of saying, "I think I'll arrive at My time, not yours. It may be midnight. Your task is to wait—and be prepared. I'll show up whenever I please. Besides, I want to see how you react. And I want to see if you had enough sense to bring extra oil."

God is never in a hurry. Have you ever discovered that? There's only one time in the Bible where God is pictured as running. That story is found in the parable of the prodigal son where Jesus pictures God rushing out to meet a lost son who is returning home. That's the only time we find God running. The rest of the time He seems not to be in a hurry. God does not wear a watch.

Patience is one of the great fruits of the Holy Spirit. Impatience comes from the pit, not from God. Everyone has to struggle with this. Wives are impatient because their husbands are slow. Fathers get impatient with their children, sometimes actually wounding them. Prisoners are impatient with their lawyers, the courts, the judicial proceedings. The wedding is scheduled for 7:00 P.M., but the bridegroom is the one who really sets the time schedule—and he may choose to wait until midnight to arrive. That's hard to take, especially if you didn't think it was necessary to bring a reserve supply of oil.

So we wind up waiting on the curb. My bottom end hurts from sitting on the stone. The bugs are biting me. A carriage has just gone past and splashed dirty water all over me. I'm in a bad mood. The whole world is against me. On top of that, my lamp has gone out, and the only one I have to blame is myself. Patience.

Jesus wanted His disciples to know that God is not in a hurry. Therefore, He said, you should be prepared to do things on God's time schedule—not your own.

"Now listen, you who say, 'Today or tomorrow we will go to this or that city, spend a year there, carry on business and make money.' Why, you do not even know what will happen tomorrow. What is your life? You are a mist that appears for a little while and then vanishes. Instead, you ought to say, 'If it is the Lord's will, we will live and do this or that.' As it is, you boast and brag. All such boasting is evil" (James 4:13-16).

In industry, in business and, unfortunately, even in churches we do a terrible thing called projection. Businessmen project sales on the basis of collected data. Industry projects production figures. Churches project financial and numerical growth. They draw up long-range plans and goals. On the basis of these, they make plans to build larger buildings.

Not too long ago a small group of men in our church in Florida did just that. Even though I knew better, I allowed myself to be a party to what they were projecting. We did certain studies on projected growth. Then a strong leader pushed through a building project. He wanted us to build an expensive new auditorium. Even though it would only seat half again what our present auditorium was capable of seating, it would cost twenty-five times more than what the present auditorium cost.

"We can do it," he said.

But when I got alone with God and began to pray—and listen—I heard God say, "You probably can do it, but that is not My highest will for this church. I want you to go out, not up."

When I began to analyze what God had whispered in my heart, I realized it was competition and image that were the motivating forces behind our plans to build. It was more important to brag about our size and influence than to do the will of God. So I announced we would not build a super-church. Instead, we would continue to build relationships and, instead of growing bigger, would help form new, small churches around the community. Interestingly, when I announced that, everyone applauded. The people knew all along the Bridegroom wasn't going to come along and bless our plans. The only way we could be blessed was to do things His way, on His time schedule.

God's ways are not our ways, and His thoughts are not our thoughts. He says, "You can't presume on Me. The only thing you can do is be prepared for Me. So bring along some extra oil. It may be a long wait. I am not interested in your schedules or projects. I am interested in people. What you become as you wait is more important than what you achieve."

Jesus tells this story to illustrate His return and to illustrate what the kingdom of God is. "You don't know when or what is going to happen,"

He says. "Therefore, it is mandatory that you store up reserves." It's not enough to be a Christian and say "Hosanna!" That's what happened on Palm Sunday as the people lined the road welcoming the Messiah whom they believed would establish a political and military kingdom. But when the crisis came, when Jesus turned out to be Someone other than whom they expected, they were caught without reserves. Their lamps had run out of oil.

The wise man understands that he needs to stay under the anointing of the Holy Spirit so that when the shaking comes there will be something left at the bottom of his container. God is constantly shaking His church. He's shaking His people. But if your face is toward God, your container will be constantly refilled. Even if your capacity is small, if you are standing in the right place—"Keep me under the spout where the glory runs out," an old Pentecostal preacher used to pray—you will always be refilled.

In the five years it took Marxism to sweep through China, more than one million Chinese people, sensing all was futile, committed suicide. The nation was a suicidal nation. They simply could not stand living under communism. They couldn't stand the crisis. They didn't have the spiritual reserves.

Now in the United States of America, as people have turned away from God, there is an epidemic of teenage suicides. Young people, who should be the most forward-looking people of society, see things as hopeless. They have no spiritual reserves to carry them through the crisis.

In 1987, when the special investigators began asking questions about White House involvement in an arms sale deal with Iran, a number of people got nervous. The former national security advisor, Robert McFarlane, a brilliant and dedicated intellectual and one of the world's experts on the Middle East, attempted suicide. He had no spiritual reserves to carry him through the crisis.

Everybody needs spiritual reserves. Jesus illustrates this by telling the story of the young women who ran out of oil. Oil, in the Bible, is the symbol of the Holy Spirit. Jesus is saying that all people need to be filled with the Holy Spirit. Only then will you have the strength to stand when the crisis comes.

Spiritual reserves also come from relationships. Every Christian should be in covenant relationship with a church and with other Christians. We need to check to see if we hold any grievance against another.

If we hold any bitterness, if there is any unforgiveness, it needs to be dealt with before the crisis comes. We should be filled with the Word of God—meditating on it day and night. The question asked by this parable is personal—and disturbing: What is your godly capacity? Are you a five-quart person, or is there a spring inside you which is constantly refilling your soul when your Spirit-level goes down?

Christians need a jug of oil like the widow of Zarephath (1 Kin. 17:7-16). After she gave her last crust of bread and last drop of oil to the prophet Elijah, he promised that her little jug of oil would always replenish itself. It proved true. "For the jar of flour was not used up and the jug of oil did not run dry, in keeping with the word of the Lord spoken by Elijah" (1 Kin. 17:16). Every time she drained it empty and put it back on the shelf, it refilled itself. There was a spring in the bottom of the jar.

My friend Gene Berrey has a summer cabin in the mountains of north Georgia where our little "home church" of ten friends often goes for group vacations. Water for the cabin comes from a spring on the side of the mountain that flows into a big concrete tank which acts as a reservoir. From the reservoir the water then flows by gravity into the house, where a pressure pump forces it through the pipes.

Last summer the spring had almost dried up. Water was just trickling into the tank. That meant, when our home group arrived, we had to ration water until we could get up on the mountainside and clean out the spring, which was filled with mud and debris from the winter's rain and snow. We had to pass laws regulating the amount of water each person could use, since it took only a few flushes of the toilet and a long shower or bath to empty the reservoir.

After we cleaned the spring, the water began to flow again—in abundance. When that happened, we began living on grace, not law, for we were drawing from an unlimited source. Once again our water came not from the reservoir—which could run dry—but from the mountain.

Had there been a crisis while we were under the law, however, we would have been in trouble. Had the fireplace popped a spark out onto the newspapers on the floor and caused a fire, calling for lots of water to put it out, we would have quickly run dry. But after we cleaned the spring, the water soon refilled the huge concrete tank—giving us ample reserves.

Today the church is entering a time of crisis. There have been many

69

warnings as strong men have fallen and large ministries have toppled, some going into bankruptcy. In each case it became evident that the problem was not only hidden sin—which clogged the spring—but lack of reserves. All men sin, but those with strong reserves come back quickly. Ministries with strong financial reserves are not crushed in times of national economic crisis. In this parable Jesus is teaching of the necessity of an inner spring. It is not enough to draw water from a half-filled tank; we need a spring which taps into a mountain.

Spirit-filled people automatically refill. They don't have to be pumped up by external devices. They don't need people who come along and stroke them. They don't need to go shopping to chase away the blues. They don't need drugs or alcohol as a substitute for the Holy Spirit. They have an inner spring which refills and reproduces, refills and reproduces, refills and reproduces.

One of the criterion I have for leaders in our church is that they be "self-inflators." Otherwise they will constantly be "drained." One strong word of criticism, one rebuke from their superior, one attack from Satan and their reserves are depleted. They come crawling, hoping someone will pump them back up. I once worked with a church staff member who was devastated because he came into the office and no one on the staff recognized it was his birthday. He sat in his office all day, hoping someone would come in and say "Happy Birthday." He waited, right up until closing time, for someone to shout "Surprise!" and produce a birthday cake. But everyone was busy, and no one remembered. By the time he got home that night every drop of oil had drained from his lamp. Fortunately his wife remembered and had baked him a cake. But he never forgave his fellow workers. Two years later he mentioned that black Thursday to me, reminding me that even I had not the decency to send him a card. Tears came to his eyes as he recalled the event.

I am not telling the story to justify thoughtlessness. I think it is nice to stroke people, to tell them we appreciate them and to wish them happy birthday. (Even though the phrase has virtually no meaning, it is often the only personal recognition a person receives during the year.) But Christian leaders in particular need to have a source of supply that is not dependent on the systems or the people of the world. They need to be self-inflators. They need to have an inner spring of the Holy Spirit, "for the kingdom of God is not a matter of eating and drinking, but of righteousness, peace and joy in the Holy Spirit" (Rom. 14:17).

God wants to restore to you righteousness, peace and joy. When your joy is all crushed out of you, sit back for a little bit. It'll come back. When you're weary in body, go lie down for a while. God will restore. He restores; He restores; He restores; He restores.

However, far better than burning yourself out and then asking God to restore is to live a life of preparedness—to approach every situation so full of prayer and the Word that your lamp will not run dry, no matter how long it is forced to burn. The secret to living the happy Christian life in times of crisis and shaking is to get yourself ready ahead of time. Preparation. To gather reserves, knowing the time of crisis will one day come.

Recently our church board of directors reviewed our budget. One of the board members, a condominium developer, asked our administrator a wise question. "Where is the item for maintenance reserve?" He knew the life expectancy on our equipment. The big air conditioners that sit on the roof of the auditorium have a life expectancy of ten years. At that time they will break down to the extent that it would be cheaper to replace them than repair them. The roof itself will last fifteen years or less. Then it will need to be replaced. He wanted to know if we were setting aside money each year so that, when the time came, we would have enough reserves to meet the need.

Everyone needs financial reserves. One day his car will break down. One day his hot water heater will spring a leak. One day his daughter will be ready for college. The wise man will have been preparing for those events years ahead of time. He will have enough reserves to meet the need.

The same is true with spiritual reserves. The wise man knows the benefit of filling himself with God's Word in good times so that when bad times come he will be prepared.

Last year the ten-year-old child of friends of ours was hit by a car while riding his bicycle. For several hours his parents—and the doctors—feared he might not live. I was with the boy when they wheeled him into surgery that night. He looked up at me from his swollen, battered face and smiled. "God will take care of me," he said confidently.

Where did a ten-year-old boy come up with that kind of faith? For years his parents had insisted he study the Bible. He had prayed daily since he was old enough to talk. He was filled with the Holy Spirit. When his lamp was shaken, it proved to be full. He had reserves—and those reserves were what carried him through the crisis to healing and health.

So often I hear people say, "I've given everything I have, and my lamp has run out." In those times I reply: It's time to enlarge your capacity. If your bucket runs dry, you've got too small a bucket. Enlarge it, and then God will fill it. And He'll fill it again. Don't allow yourself to be constricted by the religious structures so that when the crunch comes you can't reach down and find your inexhaustible spring. Jesus said we ought to be like new wineskins. New wineskins expand as the wine is poured in. They take the shape of that which fills them. We ought to be shaped like the Holy Spirit.

I have a note in the front of my Bible which says: "Jamie, don't let the world—or the church—fashion you into its mold." I go back and read that every once in a while. I don't want to be fashioned into the mold of the institutional church any more than I want to be shaped into the world system.

My friends tell me, "Impossible! Impossible! It won't work! Nobody's been able to do it. Everybody is shaped like somebody or something." I reject that. I believe it is possible to be shaped like God. Otherwise we become like the foolish virgins and only have so much capacity. Our wineskins are inflexible and rigid. When crisis comes, we can't handle it.

Edwin Markham said it well:

> He drew a circle and shut me out;
> Heretic, rebel, a thing to flout.
> But love and I had a wit to win;
> We drew a circle and took him in.

Make sure your circle is big enough to include God. Enlarge your capacity. Don't allow the religious structures to tie you down.

Today's society equates financial and social security with God's security. Then when God sends a crisis and our financial or social security disappears, we often find our lamp is empty. Our light goes out when the money runs out, or when our friends leave us—for those things are our source, rather than God.

It's not enough to have gifts, Jesus says, not even the gifts of the Holy Spirit. Gifts are no substitute for obedience and for following God. That's what Jesus meant when He said, "Not everyone who says to me, 'Lord,

Lord,' will enter the kingdom of heaven, but only he who does the will of my Father who is in heaven. Many will say to me on that day, 'Lord, Lord, did we not prophesy in your name, and in your name drive out demons and perform many miracles?' Then I will tell them plainly, 'I never knew you. Away from me, you evildoers!' " (Matt. 7:21-23).

Those who use their own resources instead of depending on God are not only foolish; they are called "evildoers." The wise person ministers only in God's power—not his own.

If you use God's resources, you may not accomplish things as fast as you want, but you never run out. God never does things as fast as we want. "The problem," one man said, "is that I'm always in a hurry, and God never is." I'm in a hurry to raise my children. I'm in a hurry to make a lot of money. I'm in a hurry to build something for God. I'm in a hurry to save the world. God, however, is more interested in building character than building buildings, more interested in what we become than how much we get done. God is more interested in means than ends. In fact, the means may be the end in God's economy.

Of course, there are times when God moves fast. Those are the white-water times of life. Last year some friends and I took a raft trip through the Grand Canyon on the Colorado River. There were times when we floated lazily along through the beautiful, deep canyon, enjoying the scenery and the company. Then there were times when we hit the rapids and all we could do was hang on. When you hit the crisis places, the best thing you can do is hang on.

Recently my wife and I drove back to Florida after spending a winter weekend in the mountains of North Carolina. Driving down the mountain from Hendersonville, North Carolina, to Greenville, South Carolina, we hit a patch of highway covered with glazed ice. Even though I was driving slowly, we were suddenly out of control. Our car was headed sideways toward a snowbank. I knew that to hit the brake or accelerator would send us into a spin and maybe over the edge of the cliff. I simply told my wife, "Hang on!" Relaxing my grip on the wheel, I resorted to prayer. Instant prayer!

We were going sideways, and there wasn't anything I could do. However, when we hit the edge of the highway the ice was thin and cracked under our wheels. We broke through to the dried grass underneath, and the wheels found traction. In moments I had the car back under control, and we proceeded—cautiously—to the safety of a lower altitude and warmer climate.

There are times in life when all we can do is hang on and pray. But those times don't last long. When they happen, God simply says, "Hang on. I'm in control!"

"Put on the full armor of God," Paul told the Ephesians when he warned them to get ready for tough times, "so that when the day of evil comes, you may be able to stand your ground." Then he gives an added warning: "and after you have done everything, to stand" (Eph. 6:13).

God loves us enough to shake us to see if there's any oil left in the bottom of our lamps. He wants to know how many of us have supplied ourselves with reserves.

Over the last few years the church at large has been severely shaken. A number of people, those with inadequate reserves, were shaken out. The wise people knew the shaking had purpose. They used the time to listen. They wanted to know not why others were falling away, but whether or not there was anything sloshing in the bottoms of their own lamps. Some, realizing their reserves were low, rushed back and stocked up before going out again to minister. They were the wise maidens. Others failed to check their reserves. They, too, fell. Nighttime is coming, Jesus indicated. Now, while it is still day, is the time to fill up with reserves. The oil of spiritual power is hard to come by at midnight.

Everyone who has accepted Jesus has oil in his lamp. The wise man, however, realizing that tough times may come before Jesus returns, always plans ahead. He does this by asking God to fill him with the Holy Spirit so that he has reserve spiritual power. The question this parable asks is this: Do I have spiritual reserves? What will happen to me when crisis comes? Have I fortified myself with God's Spirit so I will be able to stand and not fall?

No one knows the time of Christ's return. The foolish person lives for today only. The wise person plans ahead.

Lord, fill me with Your Holy Spirit so I will have spiritual reserves when the crisis comes.

FIVE

THE PARABLE OF THE GOOD SHEPHERD

God Loves Black Sheep—Especially
Luke 15:3-7

The day after Jimmy Swaggart, one of the nation's best-known TV evangelists, went on public television to confess his sin of immorality and ask the nation's forgiveness, my friend Peter Lord called me on the phone.

"Do you want to know what God thinks of Jimmy Swaggart?" he asked.

I told him since everyone else in the nation seemed to have an opinion, it might be refreshing to know what God thought.

"God told me He is rejoicing," Peter said.

"Rejoicing?" I asked. "How can God rejoice when one of His best-known TV evangelists has brought shame and reproach to the kingdom?"

Then Peter quoted Jesus' closing statement in the parable of the good shepherd and the lost sheep. "I tell you that in the same way there will be more rejoicing in heaven over one sinner who repents than over ninety-nine righteous persons who do not need to repent" (Luke 15:7).

Peter was not saying God rejoiced over a man's sin. Rather He rejoiced over his repentance. Peter was right. Regardless of the rightness or wrongness of anything else Jimmy Swaggart may have done before or after that circumstance, his public repentance pleased God.

The following week I had a long conversation with Richard Dortch, former vice president of the PTL network who was fired shortly after host Jim Bakker resigned after admitting to sexual immorality and huge financial payoffs aimed at keeping his sin from being known.

When I asked Richard what he wanted to do with the rest of his life, he said, "I want to spend it helping hurting people—people who have been crushed as I have been crushed."

Once you go through this kind of crushing and come out on the other side, there is always a desire to help others who have struggled also.

Shortly afterward I received a phone call from an old friend—a man whom I believe is one of the true prophets in the kingdom of God. He is a great preacher who had discovered some things about himself which on the surface seemed to disqualify him from ministry. He was weeping over the phone.

"When a lawyer breaks the law, he is usually disbarred—forbidden to practice law ever again. If a doctor breaks the medical ethics, he is usually suspended and never again allowed to practice medicine. Now I have sinned against God. I see no hope for the future."

"You cannot use the world's standard to evaluate God's plan," I told him. "The only standard you can use is Scripture—and the Bible is full of stories of men who sinned, of ministers who sinned and were restored to ministry. Moses, David, Peter—all sinned. But all repented. God then took them, remolded them and used them in an even greater capacity.

"You are going to emerge from this situation," I told him, "preaching about a different kind of God than you have known. The God you knew was a stern God, a harsh God, a God who punishes His children when they fall. You are about to meet the real God. The God who loves His children, who helps those who fall—the God who is for us, not against us."

There are three wonderful stories in Luke 15 which tell us something about the nature of this God who helps and restores those who fall. In these parables Jesus tells us who God really is—what kind of God He is.

Like most of Jesus' parables, these stories were told to correct wrong thinking. Try to picture what it was like. Seated around Him were His disciples, along with a number of local young people. The religious leaders of the day called them a derogatory term: the people of the land. They were commoners, natives, aborigines. To marry your daughter to one of them was like exposing her to a beast of prey. In fact, the regulations of the Pharisees stated specifically: "When a man is one of the people of the land, entrust no money to him, take no testimony from him, trust him with no secret, do not appoint him guardian of an orphan, do not make him the custodian of charitable funds, do not accompany him on a journey." In short, the aim of the Pharisees was to avoid all contact with the people of the land—people who did not think it important to keep all the minor points of the law. The Pharisees looked forward to one thing alone—not the salvation of these people, but their total destruction.

Standing behind Jesus, keeping their distance but close enough to hear, were the Pharisees and scribes—the legalistic religious leaders of the day. They were offended that Jesus enjoyed being with these commoners. They began to complain: "This man welcomes sinners and eats with them."

The scribes and Pharisees did not believe God loves sinners. To try to illustrate who God really is, Jesus told the story of a lost sheep—and the reaction of the good shepherd.

As with most of Jesus' parables, He probably began His story by pointing at a nearby field where a flock of sheep was returning to the fold for the night. They had been out on the hillside all day, grazing. It was now close to sundown, and the weary shepherd was bringing them in. His sheepdog was running around the sheep, forcing the strays back into the flock.

This was a familiar sight in Jesus' day. Many of the people were farmers and shepherds. Sheep were a valuable commodity. Every Jew had heard the heroic stories of David, the shepherd, who had often risked his life by battling wild animals which attacked his father's sheep.

The Old Testament Scriptures were filled with references to sheep and shepherds. The most famous psalm began with the words: "The Lord is my shepherd." The prophet Ezekiel spoke of good shepherds and false shepherds, and severely warned against shepherds who used the sheep for their own purposes rather than serving them. Thus, Jesus' story about the shepherd and his sheep was told from a familiar base.

"Suppose one of you has a hundred sheep and loses one of them. Does he not leave the ninety-nine in the open country and go after the lost sheep until he finds it? And when he finds it, he joyfully puts it on his shoulders and goes home. Then he calls his friends and neighbors together and says, 'Rejoice with me; I have found my lost sheep.' I tell you that in the same way there will be more rejoicing in heaven over one sinner who repents than over ninety-nine righteous persons who do not need to repent" (Luke 15:4-7).

Jesus was trying to show people that God loves. Especially does God love those who have a great need for love: the lost, the frightened, the soiled, the losers and failures of this world. To get that point across, He told three stories about lostness. He told the story of a shepherd who lost his sheep, a woman who lost her coin and a father who lost his son.

His story of the lost sheep grew out of the stress created by the presence of "sinners" at Jesus' dinner table. The Pharisees were offended. "What right do you, a rabbi, have to eat with sinners?" the scribes and Pharisees challenged Jesus. "If God hates sinners, you should hate them too."

They had their basic premise: God hates sinners.

We need to begin by asking, How does God feel about sinners? The answer is found in 1 Timothy 1:15: "Here is a trustworthy saying that deserves full acceptance: Christ Jesus came into the world to save sinners—of whom I am the worst."

How many people in the world are "sinners"? Again the Scripture is very clear. "For all have sinned and fall short of the glory of God" (Rom. 3:23).

The next question you need to face is the one the Pharisees missed out on: How does God feel about fallen, sinful mankind? The answer is at the heart of the gospel. It is the thing that makes the gospel the good news. "For the wages of sin is death, but the gift of God is eternal life in Christ Jesus our Lord" (Rom. 6:23). In fact, Paul tells us that God did not wait for us to become good before He loved us. Instead, "...God demonstrates His own love for us in this: While we were still sinners, Christ died for us" (Rom. 5:8).

While this is good news to sinners, it is bad news to religious legalists who believe God hates not only sin but sinners. To accept this means you have to admit you were wrong about God and change your entire way of thinking.

You see, the big question is not, Is there a God? That's really not an adequate question at all. I have never met a genuine atheist. I have met agnostics and rebellious people. But I've never met a genuine atheist, somebody who says there is no God.

The real question is, What kind of God is He?

We tend to make God in our own image. And because we live in a world that is full of condemnation—even churches—we tend to make God over in that image. We tend to see Him as a God who is filled with condemnation. The policeman-type God. The bully-type God. The God who beats up on little kids.

We love verses like Romans 3:23, "For all have sinned and fall short of the glory of God," and Isaiah 53:6, "We all, like sheep, have gone astray." But we add pronouns: "For all you have sinned...," and "All you like sheep have gone astray."

The Pharisees genuinely thought God loved only good people—those who kept the law. Trying to convince people that God loves folks when they believe God is a cop or a prison warden is a tough procedure.

A lot of people don't understand fatherhood. Their own fathers were cruel, didn't care or were absent when they needed them. Tell someone like this that God is Father, and all they can picture is their own father. They think, If God is like that, forget it! Therefore, before Jesus got around to talking about God being a Father, He told this story of God as a good shepherd who has a deep concern for his lost lamb. Even the most hardened prisoner understands that kind of love—the love of a boy for a puppy, the love of a girl for a kitten, the love of a cowboy for his horse, the love of a hunter for his dog. You might not be able to relate to a lost son, but you can relate to a lost animal—or a lost coin.

So Jesus goes to work describing God—the kind of God who says, "I have come to seek and to save those who are lost." In another place Jesus said, "I didn't come to invite the pious. I have come to invite the irreligious into the kingdom of God."

So here we have a concept of a God who loves all people, not just the good people. A God who loves the bad ones as much as He loves the good ones.

Many of the things that happened in my childhood have radically affected my concept of God. One of those was sitting in a Sunday school class when I was a little kid, hearing the teacher say something like, "Children, don't be naughty, because if you are naughty, Jesus won't love you." I grew up believing, Yes, that's right. Jesus loves good children. In fact, we should be good so Jesus will love us.

The problem, of course, lies in the hard fact that we cannot be good. It's impossible to keep the law, to measure up to those impossible standards we set for ourselves—or that others set for us.

Whatever it is that twists the heart at an early age will shape the tree. If you grow up believing God only loves you when you're good, then you will also have to believe God does not love you when you are bad. Since we are all bad, then the love of God is impossible to attain. Since we can never measure up to God's standard, we might as well set our own standards and do whatever pleases us. So this marvelous little parable in the book of Luke is a story not just for the Pharisees of Jesus' day, but for us.

The shepherd in Judea had a tough task. The narrow central plateau of the nation was only a few miles wide. It was bordered by plunging cliffs and wild desert. Grassland was scarce, and the sheep had to roam far to find something to eat.

The badlands were filled with predators: wolves, bears and large cats living in caves and roaming the wilderness. Fierce eagles and huge hawks circled the sky, looking for prey to swoop down on and kill. The sheep knew, by training and instinct, that safety came in sticking with the flock. Even so, on occasion one would wander off. When that happened, the shepherd had no choice but to go after it.

Each shepherd was personally responsible for his sheep. If one was lost, the shepherd was obligated to find it, or at least bring its carcass home to prove how it had died. But the shepherds, like the Bedouins of today, were expert trackers. They could follow a straying sheep's footprints for miles across the desolate hills.

A number of things could have happened to the stray sheep. The sheep could have been lost because of illness. It may have developed a disease and dropped by the path. If it were brought home, it could infect the other sheep.

It may have become disoriented and simply wandered off into the desert. To have located it at night would have been virtually impossible.

It may have fallen off a cliff and died. There was no need to go back.

It may have been bitten by a poisonous snake and lay dying. Even though the sheep was still alive, there was nothing that could be done to save its life.

It may have been in rebellion against the shepherd, wandering away in search of greener grass because it disagreed with the shepherd's choice of pasture. Perhaps the sheep needed to be taught a lesson by leaving it out all night.

It may have been killed by a wolf or mountain lion. To go back and try to find it might disturb the wild animal, causing it to attack the shepherd. There was not a shepherd who would not lay down his life for his sheep.

So Jesus told this story of the good shepherd to illustrate the love of God. It's the story of ninety-nine good sheep and one bad sheep. It's the story of the shepherd who says, "I will leave these ninety-nine sheep and go off and find the one that is out there."

The parable tells us two things. It tells us something about man. It says man is a creature of absolute worth in the sight of God. The framers of the U.S. Constitution picked up on this, as did the writers of the Declaration of Independence. "All men...are endowed by their Creator with certain unalienable rights; that among these are life, liberty and the pursuit of happiness." These concepts of the absolute worth of man came from the Bible. Few cultures of the world believe this. The classic author Rudyard Kipling, for example, wrote of the Far East, where "human life is cheap."

Not only is man of absolute worth, but we are all equal in God's sight. There is no concept of levels of worth in the sight of God. Once we grasp this, we will begin to understand how our behavior needs to change. We'll not be in trouble with each other again, because love really does make the difference.

Recently I received a letter from a prisoner on death row at the Florida State Penitentiary. He had read one of my books and wanted me to spend his last night with him and then witness his execution. He had shot and killed a policeman when he was twenty-one years of age and had been on death row for fourteen years—waiting to die. Four death warrants had been signed, meaning he had been sent up to the electric chair four times. Each time, at the last minute, an appeals court had spared his life. I was unsympathetic to his plight until I met his old father and mother, who had driven a pickup truck from Oklahoma to Florida for his execution. Dirt farmers, they had scraped up all the money they had to make the trip. His wife, his fourteen-year-old son and his younger brother (who was an alcoholic) had come with them, riding in the camper in the back of the truck. "We've come to take his body home to Oklahoma and give him a decent Christian burial," his father told me.

Gradually my thinking changed. It depends on your perspective. When I looked at the prisoner from the eyes of a state prosecutor who is upholding the law, I felt one way. When I looked at him from the eyes of the widow of the slain policeman, I felt another way. But when I saw him through the eyes of his father, I realized how God must have felt.

I realized that my whole concept of the death penalty, which had been so sterile, so absolute, so black and white as I read it from the Old Testament, suddenly had to be viewed from a concept of relationships. What if it were my son who had killed somebody? Not my son who was killed, but who did the killing? How would I feel?

Would Jesus pull the switch to the electric chair? I asked myself. The answer changed my theology.

That drunken fellow who is stumbling down the street—his clothing is slouchy; he's bumping into lightposts; he's singing loudly and falls down—is he a comedy, or is he a tragedy? The answer depends on who you are. If you are his brother, or he is your son, it takes on a whole new perspective. Love makes the difference in whether you laugh or cry.

How easily we condemn or criticize those who have fallen. We see it in our nation today as some of our Christian leaders have been hung up to dry, so to speak. Their sins are out in front of everybody. My wife asked me, "How would you like it if they dug into your past and brought up all that old stuff and printed full details in the paper?"

"Fortunately," I told her, "I've already confessed most of it."

"You haven't confessed most of it," she said accurately. "You've just confessed enough so that people no longer ask questions. But you haven't confessed it all. How would you like it if every day on the front page something else—something dirty and sordid—was revealed about you?"

It is a question every person needs to ask of himself before he accuses another. How easily we condemn and criticize. Love alone makes the difference.

Watch your wife as she grows coarse and cheap. Let it be your husband who starts to drink and loses his job. Let it be your daughter who turns to prostitution to pay for her drug habit. Let it be your son who murders a policeman. Suddenly you get a picture of how God must suffer when one of His children goes wrong.

That's the picture Jesus paints in this marvelous little parable of a shepherd who risks his own life because of the absolute worth of the individual in the eyes of God.

We don't view each other that way. We have a tendency to put people on the trash heap. God never does that. Everybody is worthwhile to God.

The parable tells us something else. It tells us not just about man but about God. It gives us a picture of who God really is. He is a seeking God who never gives up on any of us.

I have only one picture of Jesus in my house. I don't like artists' concepts of Jesus—any of them. Some have little halos over the head of an emaciated, effeminate kind of person with little angels flying around His shoulders. Others are simply facial renditions. I detest them all. The only picture of Jesus I have in my house is that classic picture of the good Shepherd, with His face turned away so all you see is the back of His head and an extended arm reaching down for the sheep that is caught in the brambles on a ledge. That is the Jesus I know—and love.

In the nation of Israel the sheep wander. There are no fences. They forage for grass and range in little flocks. When the shepherd whistles or calls, they respond. But if a sheep has strayed too far from the flock, he might not hear the whistle. Lost, he may wind up in a gully, or a ravine, or up on a high ledge where he cannot get down. He is a ready target for the predators.

The good shepherd, Jesus says—and it is obvious He is speaking of Himself—always goes out to find the one who is lost.

I've always wondered about this parable, even when I was a child. The questions that came to my mind were: What happens to the other ninety-nine when the shepherd goes off to look for the one? What keeps them from scattering all over the place? Shouldn't the shepherd remain with the larger group, or at least take them with him when he goes off to look for the one?

Then when I visited Israel I saw something. The sheep in Israel seldom belong to an individual. They belong to the community, the tribe, the village. They are communal flocks. There is seldom one shepherd in charge of a flock. Each flock has several shepherds. The sheep are part of a body. A community. When a sheep strays, the chief shepherd does not send an associate to find the lost one. He assigns the associate to stay home and watch the ninety-nine while he goes back to find the stray. Looking for the lost one is a dangerous task—one the chief shepherd would never assign to another. No, he submits himself to the danger for the sake of the flock.

When the news comes to the village that the chief shepherd is still out in the night, looking for a lost sheep, they build beacon fires around the village so he can see the reflection in the sky and find his way home. They stand watch, praying and waiting. When they see him coming across the hills, the lost lamb across his shoulders, a great shout of rejoicing goes up. The shepherd has returned with the lost sheep.

This is the picture Jesus drew of God. God is glad when a lost sinner is found by the shepherd.

The parable teaches us four things about the love of God.

1. *The love of God is an individual love. No matter how large the family, the parent cannot spare one.*

I remember when my older brother died. A very well-meaning woman came to my mother and dad and said, "But you still have three sons and a daughter left." That was an insensitive, cruel statement which brought no comfort. A child has died. It makes no difference whether there are four others or one hundred others, you cannot replace that one. The love of God is an individual love, and it's poor comfort to say there are others.

I remember my dad saying time and time again, "I never can go to sleep until all the children are in." It's not enough that three of the four are in, or four of the five or ninety-nine of the one hundred—a parent can't go to sleep until all the children are in. Each one is precious. God's love is an individual love.

2. *The love of God is a patient love.*

Sheep are proverbially foolish creatures—just as we are. We have no one to blame but ourselves when we wander off and get stuck on a ledge someplace. Yet when it happens to someone else, we have so little patience with them. We just don't put up with that kind of thing. How often have I heard the phrase, "He brought it on himself." Of course he brought it on himself. Nobody ever brings it on anybody—we bring it on ourselves. There is absolutely no way I could blame anybody else for the trouble I've had. Granted, I think there are some folks out there who want to see me fall. In fact, there are some setting traps for me at this very moment. But the man who walks with God—step-by-step—will never be snared by the enemy. It is only when we wander off that we are trapped.

No man falls into sin. He walks—or leaps—into it deliberately. But even then God does not condemn. He reaches out to save. God loves the one who has nobody to blame but himself.

3. *The love of God is a seeking love.*

Most of us are not content to wait. But God is not only content to wait; He goes out to search. Again, this cuts across our concepts of God. We have a hard time understanding this.

You see, if a man comes crawling home wretchedly, begging for forgiveness, crying out that he has repented, asking us to forgive, then we have our own little ways of doing things. We assign him a three-month, a twelve-month or even a two-year probation. Perhaps we put him in solitary confinement to protect him from himself. We may punish him. We may tell him he can do this but he can't do that. We may say he is no longer fit for the ministry. We run him through a rehabilitation school. We submit him to psychological treatment. We test him. We do all kinds of things. While all of these may be necessary before he can be restored to his former place of ministry, they are not necessary for forgiveness.

God never makes His forgiveness dependent on probation. Never. It's not God's way to put anybody on probation. Oh, He may not return them to the ministry they formerly had. They may have to start over from the bottom. They may need healing and may even have to pay the state or the church's penalty for their sin—restrictions they had earlier agreed to by being a citizen or a church member. But, even so, forgiveness is always instant, complete and accompanied by full acceptance. God does not wait until somebody is perfect before accepting him.

We are the ones who are constantly saying, "A guy has to pay for his sins. A guy has to get himself straightened out. He's got to get his head screwed on straight. He's got to take care of all these imperfections. Then when he gets perfect like I am, I will place him back into service."

Fortunately, God doesn't do that. The only thing God looks on is the heart. If the heart is turned toward Him, that is sufficient for the Lord.

4. *The love of the Lord is a rejoicing love.*

85

No recriminations. God just rejoices all the time. He never holds grudges. God is the kind of God who says, "Let's put a ring on his finger, a robe on his back and kill the fatted calf to celebrate!" He simply rejoices when the lost one is found. There is never a moral lecture or a review of the sin. He simply accepts and rejoices when a sinner repents.

We, on the other hand, want to nail somebody first. Our favorite verse is not, "Neither do I condemn thee," but, "Go and sin no more, lest a greater thing come on thee."

I'm glad that some of the hymn books have revised that phrase from the song "At the Cross" which formerly read, "Would He devote that sacred head for such a worm as I." The new renditions read, "For sinners such as I."

I'm not a worm. I've been redeemed by the blood of the Lamb. I've been clothed in His righteousness. I've been adopted into the family of God and named an heir with Christ. I am numbered among the sons of God.

We say, "I'll forgive, but I'll never forget." And God says, "Their sins and lawless acts I will remember no more" (Heb. 10:17). Our sins are covered by the blood of Jesus.

I was raised in a family of four boys and a younger sister. Everyone in the family was good—just plain good. I was the one who never did seem to be able to match up to my parents' standard of goodness. I was the one who would come in with tobacco on my breath, running with the wild crowd, sneaking into the house after curfew.

I made sneaking into the house after dark a real art. I knew where all the creaks were on the steps and how to get around those kinds of things. I learned how to open doors so nobody could hear them and how to close them and put something against the latch so it wouldn't snap.

On one of those occasions, after a football game, I was crawling past my mother's bed on my hands and knees. (I had to go through my mother and dad's bedroom—they slept in separate beds—in order to get to my bedroom.) It was many hours after midnight, and I was a bit unsteady. As I crawled past her bed I felt her reach out and touch my back. Suddenly the lights flashed on, and I was trapped.

This was followed by a long, near-hysterical lecture. It boiled down to: "None of the other boys has ever given us a minute's trouble, and you have made up for them all. I've always heard that every family has a black sheep. You are ours."

86

Those words cut. They cut deep. I had a much higher opinion of myself than that. I thought I was the really great one. Now she had told me I was worthless. A black sheep. Even though she later came back and apologized, the scar was there. If that's the way you feel about me, I thought, then let it be so.

To most children, God takes on the image of their parents. If your parents reject you, then God must be rejecting you. If your mother feels you are worthless, then God must feel that way about you also.

Many years later Jesus found me, stranded on a ledge. I had wandered away and been caught in a snare. I had been fired from two large churches for my immoral behavior. The little fledgling church I was then leading was dying under my ministry. I was within days of being eaten by the predators. Then a hand, an invisible hand, plucked me off the ledge, and I was filled with the Holy Spirit. I remember coming back to my little church after being at a Full Gospel Businessmen's convention in Washington, D.C. Nothing had changed outwardly, but everything had changed inwardly. I tried to preach, only to discover I could no longer talk about Jesus without weeping. My sermons were accompanied by waterfalls of tears—because I had met God as He really is.

The more I study the New Testament, the more I discover that Jesus is genuinely drawn and attracted to the irreligious—the black sheep of the human race. He sees in them something that nobody else seems to be able to see. And, oh, what they become when Jesus gets hold of them! The rough, the profane, the fallen, the thieves, the immoral, the earthy, those of turbulent passions, those who are unable to control themselves. What they become when the Shepherd picks them up off the ledge!

Marguerite Wilkerson many years ago wrote a little verse that says:

> The white sheep are placid, and feed in quiet places;
> Their fleeces are like silver that the moon has known.
> But the black sheep have vigor in their ugly faces,
> And the best of all the shepherds wants them for his own.

Are you a black sheep? Are you one of those who has wandered off and said, "Leave me alone. I can do it by myself," only to find you're now on a cliff and slipping off? God loves you. You are accepted by Him. You are worthwhile to Him. You are precious to Him. And He has a task and a mission that only you can do.

Your wandering is nothing more than an indication that you have been looking, that the grass you have been fed has not been the kind that feeds. You haven't been wandering because you've been in rebellion against God; you've been wandering because you've never met God as He really is.

God is the One you've been looking for. But instead of finding Him, He has found you. That's the important thing. You never find Him; He finds you. He goes to you, plucks you off the ledge, puts you on His shoulders and returns rejoicing, saying, "This is the one who was lost but is found."

The ninety-nine that were left behind are no different from you. Every one of them has, at one time or another, been a lost sheep. Every one has been called into that flock by the good Shepherd. You are not alone. Every place you go there will be a hand. The hand of Jesus will be there. Every place you go He will send His hand to hold yours. His arm will be around your shoulder. His chest will be there to lean on. His finger will be there to wipe away your tears. You will never be alone. His people will always be there. And if there is ever a time when you will be required to stand alone, then Jesus, the good Shepherd, will step in and stand with you.

The Old Violin

'Twas battered and scarred, and the auctioneer,
    Thought it scarcely worth his while
To waste much time on the old violin,
    But he held it up with a smile.

"What am I bidden, good folks," he cried,
    "Who'll start the bidding for me?"
"A dollar, a dollar"; then "Two! Only two?"
    "Two dollars, and who'll make it three?"

"Three dollars once, three dollars twice";
    "Going for three—" But no,
From the room, far back, a gray-haired man
    Came forward and picked up the bow.

Then wiping the dust from the old violin,
    And tightening the loosened string,
He played a melody pure and sweet
    As a caroling angel sings.

The music ceased, and the auctioneer,
    With a voice that was quiet and low,
Said, "What am I bid for the old violin?"
    And he held it up with the bow.

"A thousand dollars, and who'll make it two?"
    "Two thousand! And who'll make it three?"
"Three thousand once, three thousand twice,"
    "And going, and gone," said he.

The people cheered, but some of them cried,
    "We do not quite understand"
"What changed its worth." Swift came the reply:
    "The touch of the master's hand."

And many a man with life out of tune,
    And battered and scarred with sin,
Is auctioned cheap to the thoughtless crowd,
    Much like the old violin.

A "mess of pottage," a glass of wine;
    A game—and he travels on.
He is going once, and going twice,
    He's going and almost gone.

But the Master comes, and the foolish crowd
    Never can quite understand
The worth of a soul and the change that's wrought
    By the touch of the Master's hand.
                      —Myra Brooks Welch

Lord, help me to see my worth in Your eyes. And help me to see that same worth in those around me.

SIX

THE PARABLE OF THE SOWER AND THE SEED

Getting Ready for Better Things
Matthew 13:1-23

Those are eight parables found in Matthew 13. All share the same theme: the kingdom of heaven (also called the kingdom of God). These "kingdom" parables are different, however, in that each stresses various aspects of God's kingdom. Some focus on the king. Others concentrate on the subjects of the king. Still others accent the kingdom's realm, or character. Others blend several of these elements together.

Many people in Jesus' day were looking for a Messiah who would establish an earthly kingdom—one who would drive away the hated Romans and establish Judaism in its rightful place as the government of the world. Over 150 years before the birth of Jesus a strong Jewish warrior had done that. Judas Maccabeus, called "the Hammer," had rallied the Jews to overthrow the yoke of Syria and had re-established Israel as an independent state. The Jewish Festival of Lights, called Hanukkah, is traced back to that episode in history. Judas the Maccabee was called a messiah. But the Jews knew he was not the Messiah, for the kingdom he established was temporary and soon overthrown by the Romans. Now they were looking for a new Messiah—one who would overthrow the Romans and establish Israel as the leading kingdom of the world.

Those who accepted Jesus as the Messiah hoped that's what He would do. Even though they loved Him for His character and respected Him for His miracles, most were disappointed in His continuous emphasis on a "kingdom within" rather than an earthly kingdom.

The parables found in Matthew 13 show how the kingdom was (and is) to enter and spread through the entire world first. Only then would come the climax.

The parable in Matthew 13:1-23 (also found in Mark 4:1-20 and Luke 8:4-15) is the most revealing of all Jesus' parables with regard to how the kingdom will shape up, who will oppose it, how people will enter presumptuously and then fall away, and who will remain and bear fruit. This parable will give you a firm understanding as to what to expect as the gospel takes root in your own life.

The parable comes from the world of farming. All of Jesus' parables had some common point of interest so the people could identify. He told stories about sheep and shepherds, houses on sand and rock, vineyards and landowners. This story was about a farmer. But it was also about his seed. Most of all it was about the soil.

Picture Jesus sitting with His disciples around Him and a much larger crowd behind them. He points to a nearby field where a farmer is walking the furrows, sowing seed in newly plowed ground. Then He tells His parable.

"A farmer went out to sow his seed. As he was scattering the seed, some fell along the path, and the birds came and ate it up. Some fell on rocky places, where it did not have much soil. It sprang up quickly, because the soil was shallow. But when the sun came up, the plants were scorched, and they withered because they had no root. Other seed fell among thorns, which grew up and choked the plants. Still other seed fell on good soil, where it produced a crop—a hundred, sixty or thirty times what was sown. He who has ears, let him hear" (Matt. 13:3-9).

It has been said that all great teaching begins with the here-and-now in order to get people to the there-and-then. If a teacher wants to teach people about things they don't understand, he must begin by teaching about things they do understand.

The concept of the parable is that it starts with materials at hand to which everyone can relate. Then, within its own scope of experience, the parable leads the listener on to things he does not understand.

The teacher, of course, understands certain things the student does not understand. The teacher's purpose is to take that student from where he is to where the teacher wants him to be—with the hope that the student then will go much further on his own.

We see this in the academic classroom constantly. Here is a teacher of physics or engineering or architecture who has mastered the principles of his particular field. He has a bunch of bright young students who are interested in physics or whatever his field may be. He teaches them the principles of that subject, and they graduate. These are followed by another group of bright young students who, like the first class, are fertile ground into which he sows his seeds of knowledge and wisdom. After learning the principles of his subject thoroughly, they, too, graduate. The teacher may remain at the university many years, teaching, teaching, teaching. There are those teachers who combine teaching with learning, who through constant research, experimentation and involvement in their subject broaden their own minds. But often the academic teacher becomes extremely stuffy because he never goes beyond his own limited scope. Many teachers stopped learning years ago. Now all they do is communicate—often very well—the material they have. Many times the one who teaches Algebra I never does teach Algebra II, much less progress to Calculus. Why? Because that is not his field. He may understand those principles, but he has not allowed his mind to go on.

The teacher of mechanical engineering may teach on the principles of mechanical engineering, but he seldom builds a bridge. He knows all the principles of bridge-building, but his practice is limited to the classroom. I remember talking to a young man who graduated from MIT with a degree in architecture. He was talking about the fact that the professor in his master's course admitted he had never picked up a hammer. He was an architect, but all he knew was to tell other people where to hammer. He knew how to design, how to draw, but he had never gotten out there and done any carpentry. As a result, he was a much poorer man in his knowledge. Although he knew the principles, he didn't know the practical application of them.

The great teachers are those who move with their students, who not only teach but at the same time apply the things they teach. They are the ones who put into practice that which they are teaching. They learn and grow along with their students.

My professor of Christian ethics at Southwestern Baptist Theological Seminary, T.B. Maston, taught a course in applied ethics. He not only taught race relations in an era when blacks and whites were separated by law, but once a week he took his all-white class into the black ghetto where they could get the feel of what it was like to live as an oppressed people. He forced us to drink from the water fountains that said "Colored only." We used the filthy public restrooms that were marked "Colored." We went into the homes and ate meals with the black families. We walked the streets and heard the taunting remarks from white punks: "Nigger lover!" Dr. Maston felt it was folly to teach ethics and not live what you taught. His classes were small—and his class on applied ethics was his smallest. But he changed a generation of Baptist preachers, and through them changed a generation of Baptist churches, so that when he died in 1988 at the age of ninety, almost every Baptist church in the nation was integrated.

The purpose of the parable is to start where we are and describe something that is very commonplace to us in order to teach us the deeper things the teacher has in mind. But the teacher can never teach that depth until he experiences it himself. Working on the academic level is never sufficient. Practical application is mandatory.

Jesus taught in parables for another reason also. Pure truth is usually unpalatable. People resist pure truth as they resist pure medication. Medication often has to be mixed with other ingredients so the body will accept it. Many teachers—preachers in particular—feel their task is to speak truth to people. But I have discovered, after years of trying to speak truth to people, that folks simply will not receive pure truth. You cannot tell a person, "This is what you must do." The only thing you can do is put him in a position where he can discover truth for himself.

I see the church as a greenhouse. The pastor's job is to be the "keeper of the gauges." His job is to walk through the greenhouse and make sure the temperature isn't too high or too low, that the water sprinklers come on at the proper time. He checks on the plants to be sure the ivy isn't taking over all the other plants, that the cactus is not growing up too big, that each plant is occupying its own space and performing its given role. He does a little pruning and a little fertilizing, digs around each bush to be sure the soil is OK, sprays for bugs and eventually harvests.

But the pastor doesn't cause anything to grow. Each plant has to grow at its own speed. Each plant has to occupy its own space. The best the pastor can do is provide the atmosphere where you, the plant, can hear God. Where you can find God. Where God can speak to you. That takes a long time. It's not as simple as some leaders would like, those who would come storming in and say, "OK. Here is truth. Take it! Open your mouth, stuff it in, close it and hold your lips shut until you swallow it."

My mother used to do that to me until I learned the marvelous trick of stuffing things in the back sides of my mouth, like a chipmunk hides nuts, until she had left the room. At that time I could spit it into my napkin and stuff it in my pocket until I could get to the bathroom and flush it down.

Most of us do that with stuffed truth when it comes our way. We put it into our mouths, we smile, and we let the preacher or teacher know that we have now received what he has said, but the moment he is gone—whoof! And off we go into our normal way of living.

The best teachers—and Jesus, of course, was the best teacher—bring us to the dinner table and sit us down. They make it so attractive that when their backs are turned, the kids will eat this stuff. In fact, they will eat it thinking they are fooling the teacher by eating it. My mother finally, many years later, learned to disguise her horrible stuff in something called "souffle" or "casserole" with bread crumbs on top. We'd dig in, and before we knew it we would have eaten all those vegetables we refused to eat otherwise. And we thought we'd gotten away with something.

Truth not discovered firsthand remains secondhand. It remains external. Furthermore, unless we discover the truth for ourselves, we will almost invariably forget it right away. It will come in, and it will go right out.

I can't tell you the amount of good stuff that I have forgotten because it never became mine. The things that are mine are with me. The things that I've experienced are with me. The things that I have worked out in my life are mine. I may not practice them, but they are still there, and in moments of crisis they appear.

With that kind of background let us look at this marvelous parable in Matthew 13. Here is the picture. Jesus and His disciples are up in the northern Galilee region. Jesus had done what He often did—He turned the boat into a pulpit. He pulled the boat up along the shore and stood up in the front of the boat. It gave Him a little platform to stand on. The people were milling around on the shore.

It was planting time, and in a nearby field was a farmer. Around his neck he had a cloth bag which contained seed. As he walked he reached into the bag, scattering seed in all directions. Jesus pointed to him and told this little story: "A farmer went out to sow his seed. As he was scattering the seed, some fell along the path, and the birds came and ate it up..." (vv. 3-4).

It is important to visualize the scene in our minds. He took something so familiar to them and used it to reveal truth. That is using the here-and-now in order to get His listeners into the there-and-then.

When Jesus finished, His disciples were curious but confused. Jesus then went on to explain the meaning of the parable.

"When anyone hears the message about the kingdom and does not understand it, the evil one comes and snatches away what was sown in his heart. This is the seed sown along the path. The one who received the seed that fell on rocky places is the man who hears the word and at once receives it with joy. But since he has no root, he lasts only a short time. When trouble or persecution comes because of the word, he quickly falls away. The one who received the seed that fell among the thorns is the man who hears the word, but the worries of this life and the deceitfulness of wealth choke it, making it unfruitful. But the one who received the seed that fell on good soil is the man who hears the word and understands it. He produces a crop, yielding a hundred, sixty or thirty times what was sown" (Matt. 13:19-23).

The Word of God

Although the heading in many Bibles calls this the parable of the sower, it is really the parable of the soils. Jesus talks about four different kinds of soils: hard dirt, rocky ground, soil with briars on it and good earth. Each soil is indicative of the hearts of men.

It is also the parable of the seed. The seed represents God's Word, which is constantly sown in our hearts by the Holy Spirit. As we read the parable, we find the seed does not always take root. There are a number of different reasons for this—primarily the condition of the soil. However, it is important to remember that while the soil may fail, the seed is still good seed; even if it does not take root in our hearts for the reasons listed in the parable, it will still take root someplace. God's Word, Isaiah promised, "will not return to me empty, but will accomplish what I desire and achieve the purpose for which I sent it" (Is. 55:11).

The Word of God, which is represented by the seed, falls on four kinds of soils. We see these four kinds of soils in our own hearts. It is not just that there is one person who is stony-hearted. All of us have stony hearts. All of us have areas where the soil is good and prepared. So the parable represents four different facets of all of us.

The Hard Heart

The path through the field where the sower is walking is almost as hard as cement. Fields in Jesus' day were cultivated in long narrow strips, and the ground between the strips was always a right-of-way, a common path that the sower walked along, beaten hard by generations of feet passing over it. The sower, whether sowing barley, oats or wheat, is not putting it in the ground seed by seed. He is broadcasting the seed, throwing it out. As he sows, some of the seed falls on the hard, beaten path. Jesus said that this seed represented those who hear a message about the kingdom of God and don't do anything about it. Very quickly the birds (who represent Satan) come along and eat it up.

A lot of people are like this. They are unable to receive truth when it drops into their lives. Few things are as tragic as the closed mind, where truth never takes root because the soil never changes in consistency. One of the wonderful things the Holy Spirit did to me was to broaden my narrow mind to receive truth. To be pitied are those who refuse to read the Bible for themselves, but take someone else's interpretation. Jesus wants us to be soft enough to receive truth. Don't worry about being poisoned; even a cow has enough sense to spit out the sticks and swallow the grass.

97

I constantly deal with folks who close their minds to arguments for truth. They won't even look at it. Not only that, they are terribly afraid they may be polluted by something, so they harden their minds even more. They won't read certain books because they are afraid the author may pollute them. They won't listen to certain people for fear that person might change their minds.

God says: "Open your mind to truth. You are going to get old and narrow and crochety if you don't. You've got to keep your mind open to keep the zipper from rusting. So keep stretching your spiritual and intellectual horizons. Stay open to truth—even that which may wear strange clothing or be spoken by an odd or antagonistic messenger."

When the Holy Spirit is functioning in your life in His discerning mode, you don't have to be afraid of hearing people who may see things from a different perspective. He will give you the ability to separate that which is false from that which is true. He will give you the ability, as the old preacher used to say, to spit out the bones and swallow the meat. (Of course, the Holy Spirit will never contradict the Bible, the Word of God.) That is why it is so important to study the Bible continually and immerse ourselves in the truths we find there.

God's truth is everywhere. It's the closed mind that Jesus was striking at. He was striking against it in the pharisaical Jews, who said, "We know truth." Truth to them was encapsulated inside the law. They were the protectors of the law. Therefore, it was their concept of truth. They would not hear anybody else.

When they found Jesus plucking grain on the Sabbath, they called Him a heretic. He wasn't a heretic. He was trying to expand their minds. He was showing them that the law concerning the Sabbath had been written to help them, to serve them, not for them to serve the law. They thought they understood truth, but it was only their narrow concept of truth. It was truth which had been walked on, back and forth, across the centuries by their forefathers and others who had no other purpose than to harden the ground rather than plow it. The soil had become like concrete.

The Stony Heart

Other seed, Jesus said, fell on rocky soil. Rocky soil is not hard to find in Israel. I remember my wife's comment after her first trip to the Holy Land: "I can understand why the Bible says Jacob used a rock for a pillow [Gen. 28:11]. What else would he use? That's all Israel is—rocks."

Israel is a tough place to farm. History records that on several occasions invading hosts, such as the Babylonians and later the Turks, so hated God and His people, the Jews, that they cut down every tree in the land. In some instances they even salted the earth—pouring salt on the ground to destroy it so it would never raise anything. Most of Israel's topsoil has been blown away by centuries of hot winds with no vegetation to hold it in place, much less to decay and create new soil. The soil that remains, except in the Jezreel and Jordan valleys, is basically dust blown in from someplace else. So much of the seed falling on this rocky soil sprouts quickly; then, since there is no place for it to put down roots, it just as quickly dies in the withering sun.

Jesus had this kind of soil in mind when He said some seed fell on rocky soil. In Israel men have worked for generations picking rocks out of the fields, using them to build fences, terraces and houses. The seed that falls on rocky soil may be wedged in a crack under a rock. A little dust may blow over it. It sprouts, but there is no way for it to take root, no way for the roots to receive nourishment, no way to draw moisture from the soil. So it dies as soon as the sun comes out. Then it withers and blows away.

Jesus says there are a lot of people like that. They receive truth, and it begins to take root. But since it is not nourished, since the soil it falls into is shallow and stony, it quickly dies.

I look at my own life and say, "O God, so much of me is like this. So shallow. I hear. I receive. I get so enthusiastic about something. I begin to put out sprouts. Then the sun comes out and I wither. All those good intentions are somehow lost."

Across my years I have seen so many good plans, birthed in the enthusiasm of God's people, sprout up and die overnight. There wasn't enough root system to support life. I recall those early days when the Holy Spirit was moving so beautifully in our lives and we would rush into these marvelous schemes. Sometimes we'd even put money into them. Everybody would get excited. Then the sun would come and beat upon us, and we'd find there wasn't enough root system to sustain us. We had not made sufficient plans. We had not considered the consequences. We had not consulted history or thought of the future. We acted only on today. And when the dust had settled, all that was left was a withered sprout, brown and dead in the scorching sun of reality.

Jesus says to beware of spiritual enthusiasm that doesn't have a root system with it.

The Bible calls those who accept God's truth then turn away from it "backsliders." God warned the early Israelites of these dangers when He said: "Be careful that you do not forget the Lord your God, failing to observe his commands, his laws and his decrees that I am giving you this day. Otherwise, when you eat and are satisfied, when you build fine houses and settle down, and when your herds and flocks grow large and your silver and gold increase and all you have is multiplied, then your heart will become proud and you will forget the Lord your God, who brought you out of Egypt, out of the land of slavery" (Deut. 8:11-14).

The Cluttered Life

The third batch of seed fell among thorns. Thorns, Jesus said, represent the worries of this life and the deceitfulness of wealth. The thorns quickly choke the life out of the new little plants. This is the saddest of all the experiences. The others are tragic to some degree, but to see a person deliberately choose the wrong value system—rejecting the kingdom of God for the kingdom of this world—can be described in no other word than sad.

How sad it must have been when Jesus replied to that wealthy young man who said, "Good teacher...what must I do to inherit eternal life?" (Mark 10:17). He gave him a very simple formula: love God more than self. Just love God with everything you have. But when the man argued that he was a "good" man who kept the law, Jesus then applied the principle of the sin of the cluttered life. "One thing you lack....Go, sell everything you have and give to the poor, and you will have treasure in heaven. Then come, follow me" (v. 21).

In other words: "Rid your field of the briars that grow up and choke. Your briars are the most important things in life to you. Dig those things out." But the man turned and walked away. He was possessed by his possessions.

It is easy to follow Jesus until it costs us something. No man wants to get rid of his briars. But to follow Jesus means laying down everything and seeking first the kingdom of God—for we cannot serve God and money.

I constantly struggle with the rightness and wrongness of material possessions. Even though I do not believe it is sinful to be rich, I have seldom seen a rich man who loved Jesus more than his riches. Instead, over and over I have seen men and women turn their backs on Jesus' command to feed the hungry and bless the poor in order to hold on to their money.

Occasionally someone will make me an offer which could provide me with a lot of money. All I have to do is compromise a few of my principles, lower some of my standards, disobey God just a little. I struggle with these things, but I'm determined I'll not let the brambles ensnare me. I know if I get tangled up with them I'll lose a lot of skin trying to get loose. I need to be on guard all the time against what Jesus called "the deceitfulness of wealth." There is nothing wrong with wealth as long as you understand that it is deceitful. But the very nature of its deceitfulness is to fool you into thinking it's OK to lay up riches and say to yourself, Eat, drink and be merry.

Jesus equates the "deceitfulness of wealth" with "the worries of this life." The two go hand in hand. You can't have money without worry. If you don't have it, you worry. If you've got it, you worry that you might not have it some day. The whole concept of materialism is tied up with worry and anxiety. Jesus calls these brambles and briars, designed by Satan to choke and prevent productivity.

Spiritual Fruit

The final batch of seed fell into good soil. Jesus said good soil represented a man who heard the Word and understood it—letting it take root until it produced a crop.

Good soil is soil that has been plowed.

It's easy to tell if a heart has been plowed or not. The plowed heart is soft and receptive. It is sensitive to the needs of others. It is tender toward the helpless and hopeless. It knows the pain of the plowshare.

I'm around a lot of people who have never had the plow put into their lives. They've grown hard and stern. They know the answers. They storm through life hard and insensitive. Seeds just bounce off them like marbles on concrete, ricocheting in all directions. Such people are never your friend.

But take me to a man who has been plowed or a woman who has been

101

broken. Put me in the presence of somebody who has been softened by this life, who has been crushed by the experiences and circumstances of this life, and I will show you a person receptive to God and God's truth. He or she is what Jesus calls "fertile ground."

Good soil is soil that has been softened by the plow. The unplowed man knows all the answers even before you ask the questions. He is always right and is hard and stern in his rightness. The plowed man has been broken. Crushed. Sweetened. Prepared. There is no other way to have a prepared heart than to go through the crusher. But once that happens, once the plow has dug in and the soil has been turned over, then your heart is prepared for God's seed.

Isn't there an easier way to get to God than through suffering? some ask. Well, I guess if there were, He would have told us. Instead, Jesus said, "The only way to get to Me is by picking up your cross daily and following Me." There is no other way.

One of the signs of the messianic age, Isaiah said, is that the desert will bloom. This is now happening in Israel. Innovative Israeli biologists and agronomists have literally transformed the bad soil of the desert into good soil which receives seed and produces magnificent crops. Nowhere is it more evident than in the Arabah, the rift basin far below sea level near the Dead Sea. Agriculture experts have developed a process of removing the salt from the soil. Then the rocks and thorn seeds are removed. Finally it is plowed and fertilized, seed is planted, and through an ingenious process known as drip irrigation, it is watered.

The result is a wonderful harvest of all kinds of vegetables and fruit. Poor soil has become blessed soil, and the desert is blooming.

Jesus closed His parable with a wonderful promise of seed that produces other seed—a hundred, sixty, thirty times more than was sown. One apple may produce five seeds. But if just one of those seeds is planted in good soil, it will produce not another apple, but an apple tree which across a lifetime may produce more than 100,000 apples. If each apple has five seeds, this means one seed produces half a million seeds—each of which is capable of producing another half-million seeds.

The same is true, even more so, when a prepared heart receives the seed of the Word of God and lets God do His good work, in His good way, in that life.

Several years ago I wrote a book about a group of missionary pilots known as the Jungle Aviation and Radio Service (JAARS), the flying arm of Wycliffe Bible Translators. I spent a great deal of time flying over the jungles of this earth in small airplanes. We landed on tiny dirt and grass airstrips next to remote Indian villages in Papua, New Guinea, and the Philippines. We flew float planes off the Amazon River and its tributaries. I developed a deep love and respect for these dedicated men who had sacrificed much and risked their lives to fly missionaries and supplies into some of the most inaccessible regions on earth.

One pilot in Ecuador had recently been in a crash which involved a passenger in the plane. The wheels of the heavily loaded Cessna 206 had barely left the wet jungle airstrip when the passenger, sitting in the co-pilot's seat, panicked. The pilot had the throttle pushed all the way to the firewall. He had done this many times before and was confident they would clear the huge trees towering at the end of the little airstrip.

The passenger, an American who had been visiting the Indians, had never taken off from a jungle airstrip. Looking up, all he could see were the onrushing trees filling the windshield. Why doesn't the pilot pull back on the controls? he thought in terror. Fearful they were going to crash, he tried to help. He grabbed the wheel and pulled back, trying to help the plane clear the tall trees looming at the end of the strip.

But it doesn't work that way. You have to build up airspeed before you point the nose skyward. Otherwise the plane will stall.

The airplane pitched up, lost critical airspeed and began to settle toward the jungle below. The pilot wrenched the controls back and tried desperately to get the nose down. But it was too late. As the airplane reached stalling speed, the heavy engine pulled the nose over sharply, and the craft spun to earth.

By God's grace, no one was killed. But all were injured, including the two passengers in the back seat. The pilot suffered the greatest injuries. Another plane was on the ground at the strip, waiting to take off behind the first plane. That pilot rescued the injured ones and made two flights back to the base to a small jungle hospital, where they all eventually recovered.

It's hard to keep our hands off the controls. God plants a seed in our lives. What a tendency there is to dig it up and see how it is doing, or, once the plant sprouts, to tug at the tender sprout to pull it quickly into maturity. So many of us, thinking God isn't climbing fast enough, try to help Him out. We're concerned He isn't in enough of a hurry. It never works. Even the Lord Jesus had to submit to His Father's flight plan.

"Not my will but Yours be done."

It's always best to leave the controls in the hands of the pilot and follow His commands to the letter. Good seed plus good ground and a faithful sower will always produce a harvest.

That's the reason Jesus closed this parable by saying, "He who has ears to hear, let him hear."

Not only must you hear, but you must act on what He says. Not only should you be a teacher, but you should be a student as well. You must practice what you hear from God, translating truth into action.

In Romans 2 Paul talks about the difference between hearers and doers. God is calling for leaders who do more than gather hearers around them. These are the ones whose egos demand they be surrounded by hearers (or viewers). But the Scripture says unless we develop disciples, unless we ourselves do what we preach, we are empty—soundless bells and empty vessels.

The true leader is never satisfied to have folks just sit and hear. The true leader is one who is constantly saying: Transfer your hearing into doing. Move it beyond the theoretical into the practical stage. That is threatening to the teacher, because the doer eventually will leave the teacher. He won't stay in the class. He will disappear. He will be out doing, teaching others. He may come back for a reunion every once in a while. But he will not just simply sit around the feet of the teacher, saying, "Oh, that's wonderful, teacher." He will be translating truth into action.

That, I believe, is the real meaning of what Jesus was saying about hearing. The marvelous thing about seed is that one seed will produce a hundred. One kernel of corn will produce a whole stalk, which will produce hundreds of kernels of corn which will not only feed, but will in turn reproduce more corn.

Father, Your Word remains alive. Take us from where we are to where You want us to be. In Jesus' name, amen.

SEVEN

THE PARABLE OF THE GOOD SAMARITAN

Who Is My Neighbor?
Luke 10:25-37

It began with a question, the kind of question asked by those who don't want an answer. It was asked by someone who thought he knew the answer. The one asking the question was a religious Jew, an expert in the Law of Moses. Such men were sometimes called lawyers, sometimes called scribes. They were people who had mastered the Jewish law recorded in the first five books of the Bible, or Torah.

"What must I do to inherit eternal life?" the man asked Jesus (Luke

10:25). Actually he was testing Him, Luke says. Jesus answered by asking a question, "What is written in the Law?" (v. 26).

The religious Jew answered by quoting two Old Testament scriptures. The first was from Deuteronomy 6:5: "Love the Lord your God with all your heart and with all your soul and with all your strength." The second was from Leviticus 19:18: "Love your neighbor as yourself."

Jesus commended the man but added a touch of sarcasm. He knew the man was not interested in the truth; he was only trying to trap Jesus by forcing Him to give an answer that went against the Old Testament law. Thus, after the expert had answered correctly, using scriptures from the Torah, Jesus nailed him. "It's not enough to answer correctly if you want eternal life," He said in essence. "You must do the law—not just quote it—in order to live."

Backed into a corner, the religious Jew knew Jesus had put him on the spot. But he was not finished yet. The law said, "Love your neighbor." This man, though, loved no one because the law did not tell him to love any specific person. So he lashed back with a loaded question—a question designed so the lawyer could say "Gotcha!" when Jesus answered wrongly.

"And who is my neighbor?" he asked (v. 29).

One can almost hear Jesus chuckling, "I thought you would never ask." In answer to the man's question He tells the most perfect short story ever told—the parable of the good Samaritan.

As a point of interest it should be noted that in the very beginning of history God never asked questions. He spoke directly, and man spoke back directly. There was no need for questions for there was no sin in the world. Everything was perfectly clear. It was not until sin entered the world that God began asking man questions. The first question came immediately after Adam sinned: "Where are you?" God asked Adam (Gen. 3:9).

Ever since Satan brought darkness into the world by tempting Eve to question God's authority, mankind has been walking in confusion—asking questions. For centuries the Jews had been debating the question concerning whom to love and whom not to love. The result: Many of them did not love anyone with whom they did not agree. God knew this when He asked Adam's son Cain, "Why are you angry? Why is your face downcast? If you do what is right, will you not be accepted?" (Gen. 4:6-7).

The question this religious Jew asked was similar in nature to the rhetorical question which Cain, after he had killed his brother, Abel, arrogantly asked God: "Am I my brother's keeper?" (Gen. 4:9).

Cain was defending himself for murdering his brother. The religious Jew was defending himself for not loving his neighbor.

Jesus had confirmed the Jew's answer that to have eternal life you should love God and love your neighbor. Now Jesus was getting ready to point out that you cannot love God unless you love your neighbor. The apostle John later repeated this several times in 1 John 3:11,14,16.

The popular Jewish teaching of the day was to love your neighbor but hate your enemy (Matt. 5:43). John, however, said it was impossible to love God and not love each other (1 John 1:6-7).

Thus, the whole concept of this particular story deals with one question: Who is my neighbor? It deals with social relationships. Jesus had been talking with His disciples and a few others who had gathered around Him about the kingdom of God. Jesus was constantly talking about the establishment of the kingdom on earth.

"All things have been committed to me by my Father. No one knows who the Son is except the Father, and no one knows who the Father is except the Son and those to whom the Son chooses to reveal him" (Luke 10:22).

Then He turned to His disciples and said privately, "Blessed are the eyes that see what you see. For I tell you that many prophets and kings wanted to see what you see but did not see it, and to hear what you hear but did not hear it" (Luke 10:23).

I believe the Spirit of God was not only instrumental in writing the Bible by inspiring the men who wrote it down, but He was also instrumental in the placement of the stories within it. Luke, a Greek physician, was inspired by the Holy Spirit to remember what Jesus had said and to record the story of the good Samaritan following Jesus' teaching on the kingdom of God. Luke could have put this story anywhere. Had he been a novelist, he might have used it to start his biography, then flashed back to the birth of Jesus. But Luke didn't use any flashbacks, so the story comes at this particular point.

It is necessary in the establishment of the kingdom on earth to treat one another by kingdom principles. We cannot be out of relationship with one another and in relationship with God. Those two things cancel each other out. People who are angry with other people and who hate other people have just canceled out their relationship with God. That is the reason Jesus says we must not hold anger or hate or unforgiveness against somebody else. The moment we do so we have just told God, Get lost!

"Love your neighbor" means being willing to lay down your life for him. It means giving up your reputation, your belongings, your time. All these things must be shared with your neighbor. That's a tough word to grab hold of. But the Bible says that to love God, you must love one another.

It's in this context that Jesus tells this classic story. The story is classic not only because of its powerful illustration of what the kingdom of God on earth is like. It is also classic in that it contains all the elements necessary for the complete short story. It has an exotic setting. It has real, defined characters. It has conflict. It has change. It shifts scenes. It has an unmistakable moral. (Magazine writers call this the "takeaway.") Most of all, it challenges the reader to the point at which he must respond with his life—forcing him to think through the personal application. This is the perfect short story, the model for every story that has ever been told. And it's so familiar that even when we quote short phrases everyone knows where they fit in.

"In reply Jesus said: 'A man was going down from Jerusalem to Jericho, when he fell into the hands of robbers. They stripped him of his clothes, beat him and went away, leaving him half dead' " (Luke 10:30).

The city of Jerusalem sits at an altitude of twenty-three hundred feet above sea level. The city of Jericho, thirteen hundred feet below sea level, is located in the Great African Rift, which runs all the way from Ethiopia to Moscow. Jericho sits at the northern end of the Dead Sea, the lowest point on earth. South of the Dead Sea, stretching all the way to the Gulf of Eilat, is a dry desert valley called the Arabah. It is a desolate region.

The distance from Jerusalem to Jericho is about twenty miles—with a drop of more than thirty-six hundred feet. Even today, with a two-lane paved road, travel is treacherous. Cars and buses coming up that road are always in first and second gear. There are very few level places as this "Jericho road" winds its way through the very worst area of the Judean wilderness.

The road has played a critical role in history. Jews and Arabs have fought over it many times. Even today you will find all kinds of battlements along the road. It is heavily fortified with anti-tank guns mounted on the mountainsides. It is today, as it was in Jesus' time, a place of danger, a place where robbers and brigands have always found happy hunting grounds.

The Traveler

What man would venture from Jerusalem to Jericho by himself down this Jericho road? Only a fool, an egotist or a desperate man would dare travel the road alone. Wise men knew always to travel in caravans. If the elements or some wild animal didn't kill you, you were in mortal danger from the thieves and robbers who hid in the many caves waiting for someone to come along so they could separate him from his money and belongings. Doubtless, this man knew better than to venture out alone. He had probably been warned. Therefore, to some extent anything that happened to him was his own fault.

Sure enough, the fate others had warned him about came upon him. The man was a fool to be out there. Yes, he brought his problems on himself. If he had traveled the way he should have, he wouldn't have gotten into this mess. We can't really blame the robbers any more than you can blame a rattlesnake for biting a man who puts his hand in the woodpile. Rattlesnakes bite. Robbers rob. These bandits were just out there waiting alongside the road for any piece of fresh meat that would come by.

The Robbers: What's Thine Is Mine—I'll Take It

Thieves and robbers are part of the society in which we live—part of the world culture. Their sole purpose in life is to get money and material possessions by whatever means they can—legal or illegal, honest or dishonest, moral or immoral. They are without scruples. Totally selfish. Totally godless. They operate on one mentality: The only reason you've got it is so I can take it away from you.

My friend Youngblood Johnson, a former pimp and drug-runner who is now an evangelist, once told me there are two kinds of people who live in Harlem: people who make money, and those who sit around figuring out ways to take the money away from them. I told him that didn't describe Harlem—it described the entire world. The crooks and robbers in Jesus' parable are the hustlers of today whose task is to separate you from your money. Some do it with a gun or knife, others do it by presenting you with a get-rich scheme and some do it by begging on television in the name of Jesus—then misusing the money for their own purposes. All are hustlers. Thieves. All work on the principle of the robbers in this story: What's thine is mine—I'll take it.

If somebody flashes money in a crowd, there are always a number of others whose first reaction is, How can I get that away from him? If they are brutes, they will think, How can I twist his arm, or break his neck, or pick his pocket? Some Christians will go after it "for the glory of God." The Internal Revenue Service operates on the mentality that all you have belongs to the government. The government, in return, allows you to use a portion of it for yourself.

The thief mentality is selfish, since its only purpose is to get. If that means a robber has to steal it from you—he steals. If the only way to get you to buy his used car is to lie to you—he lies. The ancient Latin proverb caught the spirit with the phrase *Caveat emptor*—Let the buyer beware.

In Jesus' parable the robbers spotted the lone traveler, stopped him, beat him until he was almost dead, stole all he had and left him naked and helpless in the ditch, dying in the searing desert sun.

The Priest and Levite: What's Mine Is Mine—I'll Keep It

"A priest happened to be going down the same road, and when he saw the man, he passed by on the other side. So, too, a Levite, when he came to the place and saw him, passed by on the other side" (Luke 10:31-32).

The expert in the law to whom Jesus was telling the story knew immediately why the priest and Levite did not stop. They didn't stop and render aid for the same reason he would not have stopped. Because of the Law of Moses.

"Whoever touches the dead body of anyone will be unclean for seven days. He must purify himself with the water on the third day and on the seventh day; then he will be clean. But if he does not purify himself on the third and seventh days, he will not be clean. Whoever touches the dead body of anyone and fails to purify himself defiles the Lord's tabernacle. That person must be cut off from Israel" (Num. 19:11-13).

The priest was on his way to Jerusalem to minister in the temple. There were a number of priests at that particular time who took turns ministering there. Most had only one chance in a lifetime to perform the sacrificial rites in the temple itself. So here we have a priest coming up from wherever he lived in the low country, on his way to Jerusalem for his once-in-a-lifetime experience. He sees this body lying alongside the road and doesn't know whether the man is dead or alive.

Suddenly he is faced with a decision—a tough, major decision. Does he pause, go over to the fellow, find out if he is dead or alive? If he is alive, he will certainly help. However, if the man is dead, and he has touched him to check his pulse, he has disqualified himself for his turn in the temple. He will miss his turn to glorify God. Unclean for seven days, he will have to go through the whole ceremonial cleansing process again.

On this basis he makes his decision: The ministry is more important than the individual. He passes by and leaves him—not realizing that ministry is the individual.

Next along the road was a Levite, the worship leader in a synagogue. Levites were members of the priestly tribe of Levi—very important persons. Their mission was to teach people how to worship God. Like the priest, the Levite also stops and looks. But his motto is safety first.

As the ordained worship leader, he thinks to himself, I must be careful. The robbers and crooks could still be hiding in the nearby caves. If they're using this bleeding body as a decoy, I'm going to be in trouble. I have important things to do in Jerusalem. If I get battered and robbed by these same thieves, I can't be of service to anyone else. No, I must go on. Somebody else will come along and take care of this situation. It's none of my affair.

I know a young minister of music who was recently fired from his church for missing an important concert he was supposed to direct. His choir had practiced for weeks. People had worked on costumes and lighting. The church had spent a lot of money on advertising. But on the night of the concert the music director failed to show up. A choir member had to direct the program, much to the dissatisfaction of everyone involved.

Late that night the pastor received an apologetic call from the young Levite. He was calling from a hospital. On his way to the church from his rural home he had spotted an upturned car in a canal. Forgetting about his concert, he spent the next two hours helping the injured people out of their nearly submerged car and then taking them to the hospital. The pastor responded that that had been a noble thing to do, but that his concert should have come first. He should have flagged down another car so he could have come on to the church. A meeting of the personnel committee had already been called. The end result was the musician lost his job for "irresponsible action" and "misplaced priorities."

The Levite in Jesus' story knew something similar could happen to him, so he made a selfish choice—a choice of convenience rather than sacrifice. He passed by on the other side.

On regular occasions every Christian needs to look upon the church, upon himself and upon other Christians from the perspective of the man in the ditch. Robert Burns caught this spirit in his little poem about a man sitting piously in church, not knowing that a louse was crawling around his collar—quite visible to the people sitting behind him. He wrote in "To a Louse":

> Oh wad some power the giftie gie us
> To see oursels as others see us!

We need to see ourselves as the man in the ditch sees us—pious, self-righteous, snobbish, selfish, unwilling to get our hands bloody or dirty, more interested in our own ministry than in helping hurting people. Once we view life from the ditch, however, we always treat hurting people from a different perspective.

The Samaritan: What's Mine Is Thine—I'll Give It

"But a Samaritan, as he traveled, came where the man was; and when he saw him, he took pity on him" (Luke 10:33).

Now Jesus adds one of those wonderful twists to His story. He injects a totally foreign character. A despised character. The Jews hated the Samaritans. While the Samaritans lived in the same nation as the Jews—in an area known as Samaria—they were of a mixed race and had what was to the Jews a totally unacceptable approach to God. The Samaritans were Jews who had been left behind in Judah during the Babylonian exile. They had intermarried with the Canaanites, and they were no longer considered pure Jews. Not allowed to worship in the temple, they had built their own temple on Mt. Gerizim.

Jesus' use of the term "Samaritan" was like telling the Grand Dragon of the Ku Klux Klan who has just asked, "Who is my neighbor?" the story of the good black man. If Jesus had been speaking to a group of right-wing fundamentalists, He might have said, "But a tongues-speaker, as he traveled to a charismatic convention, came to where the man was...."

By inserting a Samaritan in the story Jesus strikes a mortal blow at racism and religious discrimination.

But the Samaritan stopped and took pity on the man by the road. "He went to him and bandaged his wounds, pouring on oil and wine" (Luke 10:34). Maybe the Samaritan was not in a hurry. Maybe he was. He had wealth, for he was carrying cash and he owned a donkey. Not only that, he had credit—enough that the Jewish innkeeper took him at his word when he said, "Look after him...and when I return, I will reimburse you for any extra expense you may have" (Luke 10:35).

"Which of these three do you think was a neighbor to the man who fell into the hands of robbers?" Jesus asked (Luke 10:36). The expert in the law could not even bring himself to utter the hated word "Samaritan." All he could say was, "The one who had mercy on him" (Luke 10:37).

I wish I had been there to see what Jesus did. I wish I could have seen His facial expression and what He did with His hands when He said simply, "Go and do likewise." I wonder if He rubbed His chin just a little, pulled at His ear. Maybe He turned and looked at His disciples, who were over on the side. I really wonder how He handled Himself as He put that last little dig in and said, "Go and do likewise."

Four things need to be noted from this parable:

1. *Very few people, even top religious leaders, love their neighbor enough to inconvenience themselves for him—much less die for him.*

2. *"Neighbor" in God's vocabulary is more than the person who lives next to us or even someone we know—he is anyone who crosses our path.*

3. *Love is shown by meeting people's needs.*

4. *The most unlikely people are often the ones who show Christian love—a fact that should prevent us from ever speaking judgmentally about any group of persons regardless of their nationality, race, religion, sex or handicap in life.*

It's the perfect short story. But it has no meaning at all unless you go and do likewise.

That we might be neighbor to those who fall among thieves, O Lord, for Your sake. Amen.

EIGHT

THE PARABLE OF THE RICH FOOL

Eat, Drink and Be Merry—
But Tomorrow You Die
Luke 12:13-21

L uke, more than any of the biographers of Jesus, enjoyed retelling the Master's stories. He spent a great deal of time writing them down. Obviously they had great meaning to him. Especially was he interested in the stories dealing with material possessions. Luke was probably a wealthy man. A Greek physician, he was able to leave his work and travel with Paul on several missionary journeys. He was also able to take considerable time to research and write two books—his biography of the life of Jesus and his detailed account of the acts of the Holy Spirit in the early church, a book which became a semi-biography of the life of Paul.

It's no wonder then that Luke was concerned with the proper attitude toward material things. He was concerned about priorities. What should a man seek first in life? Position? Financial security? Place of ministry? Family? Health? Or the kingdom of God?

Jesus told His parable of the rich fool—one of the most pointed parables in the Bible—in the middle of a long discourse dealing with anxiety. What is the thing that bothers you more than anything else? What is your most anxious point? If you're like most people, you worry more about money than anything else.

Jesus had just finished instructing His disciples, in the hearing of a crowd numbering in the thousands, to keep their minds and hearts centered on spiritual priorities. To concentrate on anything else—especially money (or the lack of it)—would bring anxiety.

Most of our anxieties are related to money. We are more concerned about money than our health. In fact, most people see money as the key to health, for if we are rich we can hire a doctor, rent a nursing home, pay for medical supplies.

If we have money we can get the best lawyer, which sometimes is the difference between prison or freedom, life or death.

Transportation is no problem if we have money.

Communication is no problem if we have money.

Housing is no problem if we have money.

Everything in the world centers on money.

Jesus had more to say about money—that is, the medium of exchange—and our relationship to it than He had to say about anything else except heaven. He also had a lot to say about money and our relationship to heaven. In fact, He said if we have a lot of money, it is especially hard to get into heaven. I've always found that interesting, because most of us are trying to get both at the same time. We want to be wealthy, and we want to go to heaven.

It all started one afternoon as Jesus was walking by a vineyard near the Sea of Galilee. Most vineyard owners planted their vines on terraces dug into the stony hillsides. This was necessary to prevent the thin layer of soil from being washed away during the rainy winter months. The vine stems grew by trailing along the ground, and once the branches were filled with clusters of grapes, the workers propped them up on forked sticks so they could ripen. After the grapes had been harvested each year, the keepers of the vineyards pruned the vines so that only the trunk and a few main branches remained during the winter.

A crowd of people had gathered, and Jesus began by warning them about the yeast of the Pharisees, which is hypocrisy. He said, "There is nothing concealed that will not be disclosed, or hidden that will not be made known. What you said in the dark will be heard in the daylight, and what you have whispered in the ear in the inner rooms will be proclaimed from the roofs" (Luke 12:2-3).

Very quickly He added, "I tell you, my friends, do not be afraid of those who kill the body and after that can do no more" (Luke 12:4). In other words, He started talking about fear and anxiety. "When you are brought before synagogues, rulers and authorities, do not worry about how you will defend yourselves or what you will say, for the Holy Spirit will teach you at that time what you should say" (Luke 12:11-12).

He had just finished teaching when someone approached Him: "Teacher, tell my brother to divide the inheritance with me" (Luke 12:13).

There's always somebody, it seems, who never quite grasps what has just been said. That's what happened that afternoon when this fellow, after listening to Jesus teaching on spiritual priorities, blurted out his silly request. He didn't even say, "Tell me how I can be rich." He said, "Tell my brother what he should do so I can be wealthy."

"Jesus replied, 'Man, who appointed me a judge or an arbiter between you?' Then He said to them, 'Watch out! Be on your guard against all kinds of greed; a man's life does not consist in the abundance of his possessions' " (Luke 12:14-15).

Then, pointing to the lush vineyard, He told them this parable: "The ground of a certain rich man produced a good crop..." (Luke 12:16).

The Hebrews believed the blessing of God was manifested by good crops. This was an agrarian society. If you lived a long time, had good crops and had many sons—sons who could tend the fields—you were blessed by God. This rich man's good crop, then, was evidence that God had blessed him—not just that the ground had accidentally produced good crops, or that the man by his own hard work and wisdom had produced them. This rich man had been blessed by God.

I often pray, "Lord, I have a special ministry project that I would like to invest money in." Then I daydream. (Some call that seeing it by faith.) I can see hundreds of thousands of dollars coming my way which I am going to give to this particular ministry I want to support. I think, God would not bless me with all that money unless He could trust me to keep some of it and use it for myself—which is probably the reason hundreds of thousands of dollars do not come my way. For I am like the rich fool who immediately says, "What can I do with what I have?"

As you read through this parable you are immediately struck by the large number of first-person possessive pronouns. "My," "mine," "myself."

I listened to a famous TV preacher recently telling his congregation that he was praying God would bless him with an annual salary of one million dollars. "I'm worth it," he told his congregation.

I have no problem with that. I think all God's people are worth—at minimum—a million dollars a year. The Bible says we're worth much more. Then the TV preacher said something else. He wanted his congregation to know that if they paid him a salary of one million dollars, he would return 25 percent of his salary to the church. How noble, I thought. But what is he going to do with the other $750,000 a year?

"That's mine!" the TV preacher answered. "I earned it, and I'm worth it."

How sad.

In Jesus' parable, the rich man's first reaction was: "What shall I do? I have no place to store my crops" (Luke 12:17). His first thought was not, "Praise God, He has given me more than I asked for; what am I supposed to do with this?" Instead he asked, "How can I keep for myself what I have?"

It's valid to pray, "Lord, I need some of Your money so that I can give it here." What you are saying is: "Here is my receiving hand. Here is my giving hand. What You give me, Lord, is going to pass through me and go into service." God loves to give money to people who do that. The problem is that I have sticky hands, and all the money doesn't get from one hand to the other. A lot of it winds up in my pocket.

Jesus is not saying it is wrong to store up things for yourself. He's not saying it is wrong to have a savings account. But He is saying it has to be in perspective with our relationship to God. We must understand that all we have comes from God. In short, a man is a fool when he thinks he has full command over his life and over his possessions.

"Then he said, 'This is what I'll do. I will tear down my barns and build bigger ones [not even God's barns—they are his barns], and there I will store all my grain and my goods. And I'll say to myself [a good person to talk to, since all this stuff belongs to him], "You have plenty of good things laid up for many years. Take life easy; eat, drink and be merry." '

"But God said to him, 'You fool! This very night your life will be demanded from you. Then who will get what you have prepared for yourself?'

"This is how it will be with anyone who stores up things for himself but is not rich toward God" (Luke 12:18-21).

I grew up believing that everything I have belongs to God—that everything I have is just on loan from God. That's not what the Bible teaches. It teaches that everything I have came from God—but it belongs to me. It is mine. But that very fact increases my obligation to recognize where it came from and that it is given for me to use wisely, for His glory.

God is not an Indian-giver. He doesn't give and then take away. He gives. It's ours. And when He gives it to us, it belongs to us. The question is, What do I do with it? It is indeed mine, but the obligations of ownership are staggering, overwhelming. Foolishness comes when I believe I can do with it whatever I want.

I have given my children certain things. They are theirs. But at the same time, obligations go with those things so that they do not have full command over them. They are obligated to some degree to the giver. I didn't put any strings on what I gave. I haven't told them they have to do this or that with the possessions. But because I gave them, my presence remains.

My father gave me a number of things. For instance, before he died he gave me a pair of long-bladed scissors, paper shears, that I have in my desk drawer. Even though he gave them to me before he died, he told me I couldn't take them until after he was gone. The day he died I went into his little study, opened the drawer and took out those shears. I carried them home with me. They were mine. But I never pick them up without thinking of my father. I never use them except in a way that would please him.

"These are paper shears," he once told me. "Never use them to cut cardboard or heavy cloth."

I never do.

Not only that, but I will never use them to cut out anything that would dishonor God—for my father was a God-honoring man. You see, even though the shears are mine, I am not in full command of them. My father's spirit overshadows all I do with them. I am obligated to use them in a way which would honor him.

So it is with all our material possessions. We have them because we have been blessed by God. God has given them to us. And even though God will not stand over us with a hammer or a whip and demand that we do certain things with them, the obligation to use these things for His glory is still there. It's OK to say they are ours as long as we understand we are part of God and part of His body, the church.

The rich fool was not his own master—yet he acted as if he were. Remember, the parable is told within the framework of dealing with worry and anxiety. The reason we grasp and hoard is that we are insecure. We think the resources of God are limited. If we don't store them up, they could run out. Hoarding is simply evidence of lack of faith.

Instead of a sense of obligation, the rich fool thought that everything was given for his own pleasure. The one thought that never entered his mind was, How much can I give away? The man's entire attitude was the reverse of Christianity. It was "How much can I keep?" rather than "How much can I give away?"

Exactly why did Jesus call this rich farmer a fool?

1. *He mistook man for God.*

He ruled God out of his life. He literally lived as if there were no God. He lived under the impression that the only important things in life are those you can touch and see and hear and taste. He said to himself, "There is no God, at least not one who cares about me, certainly not one who checks up on me, who is going to call me into accountability."

Jesus had several favorite ways to illustrate God. He loved to talk about God as a shepherd. He also talked about God as the master of the vineyard—the One who is in charge of the workers and the crop. In many vineyards you will find a watchtower, a stone platform in the middle of the vineyard where the master of the vineyard would keep watch. Occasionally the master of the vineyard would come down from the tower and walk around, checking on his workers. In this parable Jesus says God came down and walked around the rich farmer's vineyard—reclaiming everything the farmer thought was his.

As you read through this parable, the one thing that stands out above all is the rich man's unhappiness, his restlessness, his dissatisfaction with life. Even with all his money and wealth, his soul was not content. He was looking for more material things while his soul was actually thirsting for peace and happiness—the two commodities which are not for sale.

I have a friend who inherited a huge amount of money. He bought a lavish mansion where he lives alone—lonely, suspicious, filled with dissatisfaction. He has everything money can buy. But money cannot buy friendship, companionship or eternal security.

2. *He mistook his body for his soul.*

He lived as though he had full command over his body. He spoke as though all these things were his to use for eternity. That is why Jesus pointed out that where your treasure is, there your heart is also. The rich farmer had plenty of treasure laid up on earth, but not a penny had he deposited in his heavenly bank account.

Sometimes when I give my adult children gifts, they give them away. That used to bother me. Then one of them said, "Why should we be the only ones to enjoy your gift?" They've caught the heart of God. When I give them something, part of me goes with it. When they give it away, they extend my own generosity beyond what I am able to do. It blesses them for a while, then it blesses somebody else. In the process they open themselves to receive more.

Not long ago I talked to a young couple that owns a large ranch and citrus grove. They were giving serious consideration to giving the property to a boys' home. "We want to invest in something that lives on, rather than just in oranges and cows," the young wife said. "Money is really immaterial to us. If there is some way we can invest in boys, whose lives will go on, who then will produce other boys whose lives go on, who will win people into the kingdom—then we will feel we have done something worthwhile."

Rather than looking upon their property and buildings as a financial investment, they saw them as a spiritual investment. It was theirs—not to sell, but to give away.

Too many times the possession of material things brings only heart-ache. If you have money, you are always suspicious that somebody is trying to take it away from you. And they are. They're out there, and they'd like to have it all. Unless you give it away, they'll probably get it. However, no one can take from you that which has been given.

A man doesn't have to be rich to make a fool out of himself. Sometimes the poorest beggars are the most selfish and stingiest of all people. Whether you count your money in stocks and bonds or in nickels and dimes, the thing God looks at is the position of your fingers. Is your hand open, giving, or is it tightly closed around what you have?

My father spent the first sixty-two years of his life making money. Through frugal management, he not only made a considerable amount but was able to make wise investments and lay aside an ample amount for the future. However, at age sixty-two his life changed. Even though he had been a loyal church leader most of his life, he had never turned his life over to Jesus Christ as Lord and Savior. When he did that, at age sixty-two, all his priorities changed. Instead of wanting to get, he wanted to give. Beginning immediately, he spent the last twenty-six years of his life giving things away. When he died at age eighty-eight, he owned virtually nothing. He had given everything away and left this world as he entered it. Yet he had laid aside in heaven riches untold.

All we own is left behind. All we give away is waiting for us on the other side—with interest.

The rich farmer made a final mistake.

3. *He mistook time for eternity.*

He made the mistake of believing he was going to live forever.

Remember Jack Benny? He used to bill himself as the world's most notorious skinflint. He used to say, "Well, if I can't take it with me, I'll just not go." But he did go. Not only did he go, but he left it all behind.

I had a millionaire friend who married a nineteen-year-old hairdresser and died the year after. I conducted the man's funeral and afterward asked his sweet, young widow, "How much did he leave?"

"Ah," she smiled. "He left it all."

We buried that fellow in somebody else's casket. He didn't even own that. There is an old Spanish proverb: "There are no pockets in a shroud." You leave as you arrived—naked. You carry absolutely nothing with you—except the records of what you have given away.

Where your heart is, Jesus said, there will your treasure be also. If your heart is in eternity, you will plant crops in eternity. The wise man makes investments in heaven by giving money away on earth. The fool holds onto it for himself.

One day, God says, there will be a financial accounting. The rich farmer was warned. That night God was going to audit his books—and his books were not going to balance.

Pierce Harris, legendary pastor of the First Methodist Church in Atlanta, told how he decided that once a year he would publicly post the annual contributions of his church members. He said, of course, he had it planned so he would be in Europe for the two months following the posting. But on the bulletin board and in the church newsletter there was listed the name of every church member, and beside that name the amount of contribution for the last year.

He said a lot of people got mad. Some left the church. But, he pointed out, it was only those who did not tithe who walked away. Those who were faithful in giving were not ashamed or threatened. The rest simply did not want everyone knowing just how stingy they really were. It was embarrassing, he said, for people to discover that a secretary gave more than her wealthy boss, that the man who rode around in an expensive automobile gave less than the widow who was sending her son through college on a pension.

What misplaced values we have. The majority of our unhappiness comes because we refuse to acknowledge God's ownership of our possessions. What we have we hold only for a moment—then it is gone.

We should learn from Robert Burns's "Tam O'Shanter":

> But pleasures are like poppies spread,
> You seize the flower, its bloom is shed;
> Or like the snow falls in the river,
> A moment white, then melts forever.

There was once a twelve-year-old boy who had been given an assignment by his father to work in the yard. The boy hired his six-year-old brother to do the work for him. He told the six-year-old that his daddy had paid him a quarter to do the work, and if the six-year-old would do the job, he would let him hold the quarter until suppertime. The little kid worked hard all afternoon and got the job done. The big brother, true to the bargain, gave him the quarter.

"You can hold this until suppertime; then you have to give it back."

The father, a wealthy industrialist who worked seven days a week, came home late that afternoon. He spotted his youngest son with the quarter.

"Where did you get that?" he asked.

"My brother let me hold it since I did his work in the yard."

"You're holding it?"

"Yes, he said I have to give it back at suppertime."

"That's crazy," the dad said. "That's the most stupid thing I've ever heard. You worked hard all afternoon and just get to hold your money?"

The little kid looked at his dad and said, "But, Daddy, isn't that what you're doing too?"

The child was right. All we get to do is hold it for a while. Therefore, the only valid question is what will I do worthwhile with what I have—as long as I have it?

The rich farmer had power to tear down barns and build new ones but had no say-so over his life.

James says life is like a mist, or a vapor—the very best you can do is say, "If God wills, I'll be here, or I'll be there," because you simply do not know what tomorrow holds. All the money in the world cannot purchase you an extra day on earth.

For the last several years I've made a practice of going through my house and picking out something that is precious to me—and giving it away. I have to do this on a regular basis to prove to myself that I possess my possessions and they don't possess me.

If I don't do that, I will soon have to start building bigger barns to hold all my stuff so that whoever comes after me can divide it up. Instead, I'm having a lot of fun giving things away.

Speaking to the same crowd, Jesus later continued: "Do not be afraid, little flock, for your Father has been pleased to give you the kingdom. Sell your possessions and give to the poor. Provide purses for yourselves that will not wear out, a treasure in heaven that will not be exhausted, where no thief comes near and no moth destroys. For where your treasure is, there your heart will be also" (vv. 32-34).

In Luke 16 Jesus tells another parable of a wealthy farmer whose foreman was lazy, not collecting the farmer's debts as he should. The farmer threatened to fire the foreman, who then went to the people who owed him money and negotiated payment.

The farmer called his foreman a wise steward.

A steward is one who takes care of other people's things. In the kingdom of God good stewardship means taking care of the things—and the money—God has given you. God wants His people to prosper financially, but only if they are willing to be good stewards of that prosperity. Thus God may withhold riches from us until He is certain we will be good stewards; but riches are not sinful—they are blessings from God.

Nowhere does the Bible teach that riches are evil. Just the opposite. The Bible teaches that riches, or wealth, are essentially good. In Revelation John says there are seven good things that belong by eternal right to the Lord Jesus. They are power, wealth, wisdom, strength, honor, glory and praise (Rev. 5:12).

Where do riches and honor come from? King David was specific when praying to God to say, "Wealth and honor come from you; you are the ruler of all things" (1 Chron. 29:12).

God is the ultimate source of riches and honor. Anything that originates from God must be good in itself. But none of these things come if we seek them for themselves.

Rather we are to "seek first his kingdom and his righteousness, and all these things will be given to you as well" (Matt. 6:33).

> Only one life, 'twill soon be past,
> Only what's done for Christ will last.

What really counts is not how much we leave behind, but how much we have sent on before.

Father, I pray that You will give me wisdom to know what to do with what I have. I pray that You will prevent me from being a hoarder, a pack rat who stores stuff away for days that never do come. Give me not only a generous heart, but give me a vision as to how I am to spend the money you have given me. Show me how to use the material things I have. Show me how to invest my life in other people. O God, let me never reach that place where I say with the rich fool, "I will live my life the way I want: eating, drinking and being merry." Help me to remember, Lord, that eternity is beckoning me. Enable me so I am ready to die, as well as ready to live, for Jesus' sake. Amen.

NINE

THE PARABLE OF
THE TWO MEN
IN THE TEMPLE

God Listens to the Broken Heart
Luke 8:9-14

Crisis brings out the real nature of man. The way to discover the strength and weakness of a piece of metal is to put it through a stress test. Under stress both flaws and strengths are evident. If you put a person under pressure, you find out who he really is. Is his nature kind or cruel? Does he react with violence or gentleness? Does he come to pieces or exhibit inner strength and peace? Is faith merely a word used on Sunday, or is it a life lived from the core of his being?

When Job was tested in extreme adversity, the Bible says, "In all this, Job did not sin by charging God with wrongdoing" (Job 1:22). Later Job's friends as well as his wife encouraged him to "curse God and die." Job's reply revealed his deep inner faith. "I know that my Redeemer lives, and that in the end he will stand upon the earth....I will see God; I myself will see him with my own eyes—I, and not another. How my heart yearns within me!" (Job 19:25-27). He was made of good stuff.

Jesus loved to tell stories of people under pressure. He often did it by characterizing people who represented the extremes of life and pitting them against each other. In one parable He contrasted a priest and Levite against a hated Samaritan. In another He contrasted a prodigal son against a self-righteous son. In this parable He contrasted a Pharisee against a tax collector.

The story of these two men actually is the story of the two natures of man. It is a story about attitudes—attitudes in crisis.

In Mark Connelly's play "The Green Pasture," written in Negro/Cajun dialect, the story of creation is written from the perspective of an unlearned but extremely wise backwoods black preacher from the bayous of Louisiana. In the play God comes down, walks around Louisiana and doesn't like what He finds. He decides it's time to wipe out evil by sending a flood. Since He is a God of mercy, however, He first finds a black preacher named Noah and commissions him to build an ark in Louisiana. Noah is to fill the ark with animals because a terrible rain is going to come and cover the earth with water.

Then God goes back to heaven and sends His angel Gabriel to look over the parapet to see how things are going. "Gabe," He says, "how's it going?"

"It's mighty bad down there, Lawd," Gabe answers.

"How bad?"

"Well, Lawd, everything nailed down is coming loose."

God allows that kind of thing to happen ever so often. He allows crisis to come, not only to clean out the land but to test the mettle of His people. It's in those times—when all the things once thought secure are shaken—that we find out what folks are really made of.

Jesus leads into His story of the Pharisee and the publican by telling another story. The first story is about a widow who has some injustices done against her. She goes to the judge, but the judge won't pay any attention to her. However, she is persistent. She keeps going back and back and back to the judge. Finally he gets tired of her pestering him and gives her what she wants. She was not only rewarded because of her persistence, but the crisis the judge put her in brought out how deeply she felt about the matter. Jesus then points out that if the judge does that, how much more will God?

Don't give up! He says. Keep coming back to God. Not that God is indifferent to your need. No, He is testing you to see how genuinely you want an answer. God listens to His people. But He is far more interested in building character than in giving a handout. Don't give up, Jesus says, for in the struggle you'll become a man.

Following this, Jesus tells a story about a religious man—a Pharisee— who knows all the formulas for prayer but forgets God and prays only to be heard by men. In the same story is a desperate publican who knows none of the formulas and is so ashamed of his sin he doesn't want to be seen by men—but is heard by God.

Not all religion is good. In fact, Jesus said He came to destroy religion. Religion is basically a set of rules used by churches to force men into a posture which they feel pleases God. If you obey certain rules, act in certain ways, perform various disciplines, you are religious. The Pharisee was very religious.

There's nothing wrong with obeying rules, acting right and living a disciplined external life. Jesus said that was good—as long as we majored on the inner life and minored on the externals.

Religion does strange things to people. It often causes them to get puffed up, stuffy, sometimes even self-righteous. The more religious a person becomes, the more he thinks himself right—and others wrong.

Jesus loved to poke holes in the balloons of religious people who were puffed up on the hot air of their own piousness. Seeing that some Pharisees had joined the group where He sat teaching, Jesus pointed at the temple and told this story about the two men who entered to pray. It was to the Pharisees that Jesus was primarily talking, for the story begins: "To some who were confident of their own righteousness and looked down on everybody else, Jesus told this parable: 'Two men went up to the temple to pray, one a Pharisee and the other a tax collector...' " (Luke 18:9-10).

Jesus loved to draw contrasts.

Pharisee. More than 150 years before the birth of Christ, the nation of Israel was under the control of Syria. After much suffering, a small band of Jews led by Judas the Maccabee revolted. This turned into a full-scale revolution which drove the Syrians out of Israel. As often happens, corruption followed the revolution. A group of religious Jews, called Hasidim—"God's loyal ones"—separated themselves from the government and vowed to live holy, separate lives. From this group a minority, dedicated not only to preserving the law and all its interpretations but to living out every aspect of the law, exerted powerful influence throughout the nation. They were called Pharisees, or "the separated ones."

The Pharisees avoided contact with anything which would make them ritually impure. They kept all the laws of Moses as well as the interpretations called the oral law, or Talmud. By the time of Jesus they had become a law unto themselves, feeling that because they were so pious they alone had access to God. Jesus pointed out, however, that while they kept the letter of the law, they missed the spirit of the law. He likened them to above-ground tombs—white-washed on the outside but inside filled with rotting flesh and dead bones. He called them "hypocrites"— actors who wear masks to cover their real identity.

Publican. Shortly after the Syrians were driven from the land, the Romans occupied Israel. They selected certain Jews who were willing to cooperate with the Romans to collect taxes for them. These tax collectors (the Greek word *telones,* tax collector or *publicani,* translated publican—or public contractor) were looked upon with hate and scorn by the Jews, who felt they had betrayed their own people for money. Not only were they collaborating with the hated occupation forces, they had the authority to persecute their own people—often collecting twice the amount of taxes due so they could line their own pockets. This extortion—plus the fact that they were ceremonially unclean since they had continual contact with gentiles—made them a hated and despised class of people. Therefore, their critics lumped them with others equally despised by the Jews: "publicans and sinners," or "publicans and harlots."

Perhaps a little Jewish merchant owned a stall in the old city where he sold spices. He owed the Roman government, who occupied the land of Israel during Jesus' day as an oppressive government, a hundred dollars in back taxes. The Jewish tax collector had the authority to collect two hundred dollars—and keep a hundred dollars for himself. Sometimes he would keep it all and tell the Romans the man refused to pay his taxes.

They would then shut him down and probably put him into prison.

You can understand, then, how these tax collectors were looked upon by their own people. There was nothing good about them as far as the Jews were concerned.

Jesus contrasts these two men—both Jews—who came to the temple. One of them was a hands-crosser, a self-righteous fundamentalist. He had a star of David hanging around his neck and a dove on the license plate of his chariot as he pulled up in front of the temple. He carried a huge scroll, complete with maps, concordance and an encyclopedia. It was wrapped in a big leather cover with a cross on one side and a dove on the other side—packed full of cassette tapes.

Nobody was more religious than this fellow. He went to church three times on Sunday, attended the Wednesday night meetings, prayed at the men's prayer breakfast, watched all the religious television shows, gave 10 percent of his income to his church, another 10 percent to the poor and a final 10 percent to the television evangelists. He was righteous. Self-righteous.

Over there across the room was the tax collector—the lowest of the low. He had made a mess of his life. His wife had left him. He'd been to church only twice since the day he was born, and then he couldn't understand what was going on. He had just been convicted and was awaiting sentence. He was going to be in jail a long time. All he had to present to God was a broken heart.

Then Jesus talked about the prayers the men prayed.

"The Pharisee stood up and prayed about himself" (Luke 18:11).

I love the way Jesus told the story. One Bible version says the Pharisee prayed with himself. Another says he prayed to himself. One thing was sure: he was either talking to himself or to the folks around him about himself—but he wasn't talking to God.

Phillips Brooks once talked about a man who "uttered the most eloquent prayer ever offered to a Boston audience."

I grew up on prayers like this. We used to sit at the dinner table while my mother prayed long, long prayers. She didn't pray to God—at least not then. (She does now.) She was using the occasion to preach to the kids about all the things we'd done wrong that day.

A lot of spoken prayers are like that—prayed to people and not to God. You hear them in church all the time. There's the preaching prayer, where the preacher talks about God in the third person. Then there's the announcement prayer. "Dear God, bless the men's prayer breakfast that we forgot to announce earlier. It's going to be at 6:30 Saturday morning. And bless Master Sergeant Kill-Em-Dead, who's going to be our speaker that morning."

And, of course, there are the bragging prayers—the kind the Pharisee prayed.

Jewish law called for one fast a year, on the day of atonement. The Jews then, like the Orthodox Jews of today, kept these fasts religiously. But this fellow went way beyond that. He fasted every Monday and Thursday as well. Mondays and Thursdays were the market days in Jerusalem, and the city was crowded. Since the Jews put powder on their faces when they were fasting, to fast on market days meant lots of people knew how religious he really was. Very important. What good is there in being holy if only God knows? This fellow had to let a few others know, which is the reason he was praying loud enough so everyone could hear him.

Tithing and fasting, Jesus said, should be a part of the Christian life. But once it becomes a prideful thing, all meaning is gone. We are to fast unto God, not for man to notice. We give our money to God, not so men will see how much we give and be impressed. Jesus did not condemn public prayer, tithing one's income or disciplined fasting. He said those were good things. But in this parable He reminds us that prayer is a condition of the heart—not a bunch of words. In fact, sometimes the greatest prayers are those we can't voice—the ones we only groan from our broken hearts.

That's the best the tax collector could do. He didn't even kneel. He didn't know the right procedure. He just stood there before God, crying, "God, have mercy on me, a sinner" (Luke 18:13). In the original language it's even more specific: "God, have mercy on me, the sinner"—as though he were the only sinner in the world.

True repentance is never for what we've done; it's for who we are. I remember the time I heard God telling me, "I don't want to hear you say ever again that you are sorry for what you've done." You don't get into heaven by doing good things, nor do you go to hell for doing bad things. It's not what you've done that counts; it's who you are.

True repentance was exhibited by the tax collector, who was heartbroken and self-despising. He did not compare himself with anybody else, especially the righteous man who was there. He did not say, "God, I can't be as good as he is." He simply said, "God, have mercy on me, the sinner."

At the same time the Pharisee was praying with his eyes open, looking around the room and finally spotting the tax collector who immediately became the object of his scorn: "God, I thank You that I am not like...."

"God, do something with me. I can't stand the way I am any longer." God always does something with the man who says that. While God ignores the person who prays, "God, change that other fellow," He always responds when you look into your own heart and say, "God, change my heart." It's then He says, "I've been waiting for a man who prays like that."

In the old city of Jerusalem there is a little gate through the wall called "the eye of the needle." Jesus referred to this gate when He once said it was easier for a camel to pass through the eye of the needle than for a rich man to enter heaven. He was not saying money would keep you out of heaven. He was talking about the condition of the heart, for the only way a camel could ever get through the "eye of the needle" was to crawl through on its knees.

Jesus says you can't pray and be proud at the same time. I remember an old pastor friend of mine who said many years ago, "The gate of heaven is so low that a man can only enter on his knees." You can't stand upright before God. You can only come with an attitude of humility. No one who despises his fellow man can pray. You cannot pray if you have aught against your brother, Jesus said in Mark 11:25. Until we're reconciled with our brothers, our contact with God is shut off. Husband and wife who are out of sync with each other can't reach God. A man who is out of sync with his business associates or his friends; children who have aught against their parents—their communication with God is blocked.

God desires that we have a clean heart. God wants us to talk to Him about ourselves, not about others. God does not rejoice when one of His servants falls. He weeps. But if our status in the kingdom is dependent on being "more worthy" than someone else, then we can only rejoice when that someone else is proven unworthy. Therefore, we often find ourselves more like the Pharisee than the publican—glorying in another's discomfort or at best muttering a pious "Tch, tch."

God's principle is found in the tragic story of King Saul, who, having lost his relationship with God, visited a witch seeking wisdom. God condemned him for his foolish and sinful action. Shortly after that, Saul, battling the Philistines, was defeated. He realized that God's anointing was no longer on him, and in great despair he put the blunt end of his spear in the ground, the tip against his chest and fell against it—attempting suicide.

When one of his soldiers found him dying, Saul pleaded with him to put him out of his misery. Later, another, seeing an opportunity to benefit by this, raced to Saul's rival, David, and brought the news of Saul's ignominious death. Surely, he thought, David will rejoice, promote me and publish the news far and wide.

Instead, David had the soldier who had claimed to have taken the life of Saul executed. Then, turning to his people, he said of Saul's death, "Tell it not in Gath, proclaim it not in the streets of Ashkelon, lest the daughters of the Philistines be glad, lest the daughters of the uncircumcised rejoice" (2 Sam. 1:20).

It was the Philistines who rejoiced and "sent messengers throughout the land of the Philistines to proclaim the news in the temple of their idols and among their people" (1 Sam. 31:9), not the people of God. David did not rejoice when his rival fell. He wept, for his greatness did not depend on Saul's weakness.

That is the reason Jesus concluded His parable saying, "This man [the tax collector], rather than the other [the Pharisee], went home justified before God. For everyone who exalts himself will be humbled, and he who humbles himself will be exalted" (Luke 18:14).

In mid-April one year my wife and I left our home in Florida to spend a few days in our little mountain cabin in Western North Carolina. The night before we left to return home we stood on the front porch looking out at the mountainside. Winter was still in the mountains. Everything was drab. Earlier we had walked out in the woods. Many of the branches had been broken off from a heavy winter storm the week before we arrived. There was a lot of debris on the ground. There was no beauty. It was a depressing sight.

We rose early the next morning to close the cabin and return home. I pulled open the window shade and looked out at the yard and pasture. "Get up," I said to my wife. "Come and see."

She got out of bed and stood beside me. Overnight the world had been transformed. Six inches of white, fluffy snow had fallen. The entire countryside, once dull and drab, was now a winter wonderland sparkling in the glow of the rising sun. I walked out on the front porch and looked across the pasture. The night before it had been brown, barren. Now it was brilliant in purity. Every old fence post was a monument to God's creation. An old song bubbled out of my memory and danced to my lips. I stood, singing softly:

> What can wash away my sin?
> Nothing but the blood of Jesus.
> What can make me whole again?
> Nothing but the blood of Jesus.
> Oh, precious is the flow
> That makes me white as snow.
> No other fount I know,
> Nothing but the blood of Jesus.

God, be merciful to me, the sinner.

TEN

THE PARABLE OF THE PRODIGAL SON

Welcome Home
Luke 15:11-32

Any teacher who tells a story takes a risk with the person who hears that story. Jesus was such a storyteller. He knew that His stories would be received with mixed reactions. Some people would simply not understand and would go away scratching their heads. Others would misunderstand and twist the meaning to justify what they were doing rather than changing—as Jesus intended them to do. Still others would understand exactly what He was saying and react with anger—for they would realize He was threatening their life-style, doctrine or traditions. A few, however, would understand and be inspired to change their way of life and therefore become more like God. Jesus wanted everyone to respond that way, but He was wise enough to know the majority would respond in one of the other ways.

One day Jesus was sitting with a group of tax collectors and "sinners." Tax collectors were Jewish citizens who took advantage of the Roman occupation of Palestine for their own financial gain. For a fee they had purchased a franchise which authorized them to collect taxes from their own people. In fact, they not only collected taxes but, using threat and extortion, collected huge sums over and above due taxes—which they kept for themselves. In return they received personal protection from the Romans.

It was late winter, just a month before He would be crucified. Jesus was in the region of Peraea on the eastern banks of the Jordan River near the town of Bethabara. That afternoon the group that gathered around Jesus was relaxed, eating and drinking together. These "undesirables" were listening intently to what Jesus was saying about the kingdom of God. Remember, He did not teach like the scribes and Pharisees, who quoted the ancient rabbis as their authority. Those who heard Him knew He was an authority within Himself.

But the Pharisees and teachers of the law were offended. Angry. Not so much with what Jesus was saying, for they weren't listening. They were angered that He, a recognized Jewish teacher, was eating and drinking with people they considered to be riff-raff. They called them "people of the land"—nonreligious types.

In response to their anger Jesus told three short stories. All had to do with things that were lost and the joy that should accompany the finding. The first story was of a shepherd who lost his sheep. Then he told a story about a woman who lost a silver coin. His final story featured a lost son and his relationship with a loving father and a jealous, self-righteous elder brother.

The Bible is a mirror. When we read these stories, we don't see the characters in the parable. We see ourselves. That's painful.

On the bedroom wall of our little cabin in the mountains of North Carolina we have a cheap, full-length mirror. My wife often says she wishes we would bring the mirror back to our Florida home. Her reason: "It makes me look skinny."

I've seen other mirrors that make you look fat, or distort you. But the mirror of Jesus' parables is a true reflection of our spiritual figure.

The characters we find in Jesus' parable of the prodigal son are classic representations of mankind. It's the story of a family, a father with two sons. We know nothing about the mother. She is omitted from the story. A lot of Jesus' parables have to do with women. But in this particular story He did what a good author always does—He edited out all the characters that would get in the way of the story itself.

Besides the three major players, there are a number of supporting actors: servants, bartenders, a pig farmer, plus the shadowy figures of harlots, barflies and street people.

"There was a man who had two sons. The younger one said to his father, 'Father, give me my share of the estate.' So he divided his property between them" (Luke 15:12).

Under Jewish law a father was supposed to divide his inheritance after he died, with two-thirds going to the elder son and one-third to the younger. But the younger son had problems. He didn't want to wait until his dad died. He wanted his share as soon as he came of age.

While the father could divide up the "living" and give it to his son, he could not impart to him "life." Life comes only when one is reborn, or, in the words of this parable, "comes to himself." The younger son could not get that from his father. He would have to find it himself.

God seldom says no or blocks our way when we start out to do foolish things. Like any wise father, He allows us to find our own way. The possession of material things, while important to mortals, is never a priority to God. In this case the father did nothing to interfere with the boy's headstrong determination to do things his way.

"Not long after that, the younger son got together all he had, set off for a distant country and there squandered his wealth in wild living" (Luke 15:13). The King James Version says the younger son squandered his wealth in "riotous living." In other words, he took everything that was sacred and blew it.

Youth often see everything in the now. They have little past to draw from—they have virtually no concern for the future. If they have money in their pockets, it is there but for one reason—to spend as quickly as possible. The idea of investing, saving, frugality or even giving is a foreign thought to most young people. The younger son was no exception. Selfish and impatient, he could hardly wait to get away from home to spend his inheritance.

Riotous living is not just blowing it all in the disco, or meeting a strumpet on the street and giving her your new car because it goes with her long red hair and beautiful fingernails. Riotous living is basically unwise expenditures. The wife of a famous television evangelist made history by spending hundreds of thousands of dollars on clothes and jewelry she couldn't even wear. The wife of the former president of the Philippines bought thousands of pairs of expensive shoes—more than she could wear out in ten lifetimes, while many of her countrywomen were going barefoot. Wild, riotous living. Throwing away money that could have fed the poor, clothed the naked, housed the homeless.

So the story begins with a rebellious son who turns his back on his father and decides to live life his own way. In the process he loses everything he has.

"After he had spent everything, there was a severe famine in that whole country" (Luke 15:14). It's interesting how famines never happen until you have spent it all. But people interested in wild living never seem to realize that famines are a part of nature. They never seem to be able to plan for emergencies. They live as if the money will last forever. But it doesn't. Someone said, "Money talks—it says, 'Good-bye!'" If we have not invested wisely, we're in trouble.

This kid simply didn't have the ability to plan for the future. He thought money was there to be spent, to be thrown away. He didn't realize that money is a tool to be used. If someone gives you a shovel, you're a fool if you sell your shovel so you can buy food. If you keep your shovel, you can dig a ditch, earn money, buy food and still have the ability to dig another ditch for the next meal. This kid gave his tool away. He didn't understand the concept of stewardship.

"So he went and hired himself out to a citizen of that country, who sent him to his fields to feed pigs. He longed to fill his stomach with the pods that the pigs were eating, but no one gave him anything" (Luke 15:15-16).

He got hungry, and that forced him to do something he'd never done in all his life—get a job. Up until then he was simply the son of a rich man spending his daddy's money. The job was nothing to brag about. He was slopping pigs. What could be more demeaning, more humiliating: a Jewish boy feeding pigs? But for the first time he examined all the options. In this case he found only two: get a job or starve. And something happened in the job process as he went to work with his hands.

Again, the mirror is held up to each of us. The Bible has a great deal to say to us about work. Man is fulfilled only when he is working. Work is part of the purpose in our lives. Paul told the lazy Christians in Thessalonica, "If a man will not work, he shall not eat" (2 Thess. 3:10). It's honorable to work. We're created to work. It is part of God's plan for our lives.

It's easy to throw Dad's money away. But if it's yours, if you've had to work all day to earn a few dollars, you think twice before you put it in a slot machine.

When the son went to work, something happened inside him. Sometimes hardship and poverty are God's way of bringing us to the place of seeing who we really are. If you don't go through these things, you never reach the place where you say, "This is who I really am."

Those who work with drug addicts and alcoholics know that unless a man or woman reaches bottom—reaches the place where he realizes his life is out of control—he seldom makes it. The prodigal hit bottom when he wound up feeding pigs. When he did, other things—like reality— came into focus.

For the first time he was able to say, "Man, I've made a mess of things." That allowed him to see other things.

"I don't belong here. I'm not created to slop pigs. I have a better purpose in life than this. I'd rather work for my dad than for the pig slopper."

The major turning point was when "he came to his senses" (Luke 15:17).

"Senses" means he began to think clearly—with the mind of God. He thought of his current situation and evaluated it objectively. "How many of my father's hired men have food to spare, and here I am starving to death!" (Luke 15:17).

He thought of what would be necessary to change his situation. First he would have to act. "I will set out and go back to my father...." Second, he would have to repent. "...And say to him: Father, I have sinned against heaven and against you. I am no longer worthy to be called your son" (Luke 15:18-19).

When a man is able to say, "I am no longer worthy," God is able to say, "I give you My worthiness."

You don't have to change clothes to go home. You don't have to wash off the pig smell. Home is where you are accepted even though you smell like a pig. You can go home dirty. You can go home broke. You can go home diseased. The only thing necessary to go home is a heart that says, "I am no longer worthy."

"So he got up and went to his father. But while he was still a long way off, his father saw him and was filled with compassion for him; he ran to his son, threw his arms around him and kissed him" (Luke 15:20).

This is the only time in the Bible God is pictured as running—but you can see He's running to greet His son who was lost and has now returned. He doesn't stand there with His arms crossed, tapping His foot. He rushes to meet.

Remember, this story is but one story in a trilogy of short stories. While all three stories deal with things lost and found—sheep, coin, son—they are really not about the lost items but about the ones who find the items. Therefore, the first story is not about a lost sheep; it is about a good shepherd. The second story is not about a lost coin; it is about an industrious woman who does not give up. The third story, while known traditionally as the parable of the prodigal son, is actually the parable of the loving father.

When the prodigal son started home, his father, perhaps standing in the watchtower of the vineyard or olive grove, saw him first. Dashing down the road toward his returning son, the father shows us what God is really like. As the good shepherd rejoiced when he found his lost sheep, and as the woman called all her friends together and threw a party, rejoicing that she had found her precious coin, so God rejoices when one of His wayward children comes home.

Jesus wanted the people—you and I—to know who God really is. He's not a drunk tyrant with a razor strap who abuses little kids. He's not a policeman with a billy club. He's not a judge with a gavel. He's a loving father rushing to meet a wayward son—rushing with open arms.

Immediately the son started off into his rehearsed speech. However, he never got to the part about "Make me as one of your hired servants." The father cut him off halfway through the speech by smothering his face with kisses.

The kisses not only assured him of his welcome but sealed his pardon. His follies were forgiven—and would never be mentioned again. This was like David's kissing Absalom, his wayward son (2 Sam. 14:33).

"Quick!" the father says to his servants. "Bring the best robe and put it on him. Put a ring on his finger and sandals on his feet. Bring the fattened calf and kill it. Let's have a feast and celebrate" (Luke 15:22-23).

The robe stands for honor. You're going to be welcomed back into this home with honor. You left with dishonor, but you return with honor. You left wearing the clothes symbolic of the family. You return in rags—but are greeted with the best robe. Not only shall you be clothed, you shall be adorned. Instead of being told, "As soon as you're properly attired you're welcome home," the father himself says, "I'll dress you from my own wardrobe. You will wear my clothes because you are my son." You're dressed with honor because you are going to be the welcome guest at your father's table.

Next comes the ring. What kind of ring? It was a signet ring. When the son left, he was wearing his father's signet ring. It was part of the inheritance. Now it was gone. What happened to it? The son did what all men do when they run out of money and need a drink—he hocked it. He sold his inheritance for drink or drugs. But the father never questions. Nor reproves. God only reproves those who refuse to come home. Once you start that journey, however, God has nothing but welcome and commendation. Even if you haven't budged an inch from the pig pen, if your heart is turned toward God and home, God rushes out to meet you and reclothe you and re-establish your inheritance.

The ring stands for authority. When you wear the signet ring, you represent the father. Sonship has been restored.

Noticing his son was barefoot, the father called for sandals. It was the father's way of saying, "The road you have traveled has been painful. Now I am going to make it easy for you."

Later the apostle Paul said a son of God should have "feet fitted with the readiness that comes from the gospel of peace" (Eph. 6:15). This prodigal son was not saved to grow fat around his father's table. He was saved to serve. He was saved to carry the good news of a loving father around the world. "How beautiful on the mountains," Isaiah said, "are the feet of those who bring good news, who proclaim peace, who bring good tidings, who proclaim salvation, who say to Zion, 'Your God reigns!' " (Is. 52:7).

Then, turning to his servants, the father says, "Bring the fattened calf and kill it. Let's have a feast and celebrate. For this son of mine was dead and is alive again; he was lost and is found" (Luke 15:23-24).

It's a great story, and a lot of us wish it ended right there. But this parable, like the others in Luke 15, was told because the scribes and Pharisees were complaining that Jesus "welcomes sinners and eats with them." The key to each of the parables is the fact that the shepherd, the woman and the father rejoiced and celebrated when they found what was lost. Jesus expected the Pharisees and teachers of the law to rejoice also, rather than complain, when "sinners" came to Him.

However, since the Pharisees did not seem to get the point in the first two parables, Jesus added a third chapter to this last parable on the prodigal son. He described the attitude of the elder brother, which was the exact attitude of these super-religious people.

The elder brother was a hard-working, loyal, law-abiding legalist. He knew as soon as his younger brother asked for the inheritance that he was going to waste it.

"You know what's going to happen," he had complained bitterly to his father. "I'll tell you right now what's going to happen. He's going to go out and blow it all. It's going to be gone. If you give it to him now, you might as well tell it good-bye. I'm telling you, Dad, this is how it's going to happen."

Then he adopted a "wait-and-see" attitude. When the younger brother finally came dragging home, and his father rushed out to meet him and celebrate, the elder brother had but one comment: "I told you so."

God did not condone what the prodigal did. Jesus called his life-style foolish and wicked. But equally foolish and equally wicked was the attitude of the elder brother.

As we read this parable we discover that both sons were prodigal. One squandered his father's inheritance and was miserable; the other stayed home, kept the rules and was miserable. The father had to go out to them both. Jesus is pointing out that simply keeping the rules does not make a man happy. He is happy only when he has eyes to see as God sees.

The elder brother was like those Pharisees who were offended because Jesus ate with "sinners." He refused to acknowledge the boy was even his brother.

In describing his brother's activities in the far country, the elder brother gives a detail the Bible has not mentioned before. He accused his brother of associating with harlots. Perhaps he did, but the brother didn't know it. Accusing others of things they have not confessed or of things yet unproven is often more of a revelation of the character of the accuser than of the accused.

The elder brother, coming in from the fields where he has been working hard, hears the music and smells the cooking meat. "What's going on?" he asks a servant. "Your brother has come...and your father has killed the fattened calf because he has him back safe and sound" (Luke 15:27).

"He killed the fattened calf? We were saving that! That was going to be for my celebration! He has killed the fattened calf for that no-good deadbeat?" And the older brother became angry and refused to go in. He stood outside and pouted, arms crossed, foot tapping.

The father came out and pleaded with him. Twice in this story we see the father going out to his children. First to the prodigal who was coming home, then to the proud elder brother who was standing outside having a temper tantrum.

" 'My son,' the father said, 'you are always with me, and everything I have is yours' " (Luke 15:31). No, you never got a calf. The whole herd is yours. I love you and I respect you because you have stayed with me. It's all yours. " 'But we had to celebrate and be glad, because this brother of yours was dead and is alive again; he was lost and is found' " (Luke 15:32).

The elder brother had problems with that. He thought his father was rewarding irresponsibility. Neither son fully understood mercy. One was trapped by sin—the other by religion.

God is bigger than both.

God is a God of second chances. Not only to the prodigal but to the self-righteous elder brother.

All have sinned and come short of God's glory. Keeping the rules does not make us less sinners than squandering all we have in riotous living. Both the prodigal and the elder son needed salvation. God does not require anything of us except a broken heart, admission of our sin and a willingness to come home. He takes care of the rest.

Give me a humble and contrite heart, O Lord, that I may see my own need and forever turn to You, rejoicing with You when others return as well.